LORENZA'S ANTIPASTI

LORENZA DE'MEDICI

LORENZA'S ANTIPASTI

CLARKSON POTTER/PUBLISHERS
NEW YORK

Published by Clarkson N. Potter/Publishers, 201 East 50th Street, New York, New York, 10022. Member of the Crown Publishing Group.

Random House, Inc., New York, Toronto, London, Sydney, Auckland
www.randomhouse.com

CLARKSON N. POTTER, POTTER, and colophon are trademarks of Clarkson N. Potter, Inc.

Originally published in Great Britain by Pavilion Books Ltd. in 1998.

Printed and bound in Great Britain by
Butler & Tanner Ltd, Frome and London

Art direction and design by David Costa and Fiona Andreanelli at Wherefore Art?

Text with the assistance of John Meis

Library of Congress Cataloging-in-Publication Data

De' Medici Stucchi, Lorenza, 1926-
    [Antipasti]
    Lorenza's antipasti / by Lorenza de'Medici. -- 1st ed.
        p.   cm.
    ISBN 0-609-60151-2 (alk. paper)
    1. Appetizers. 2. Cookery. Italian. I. Title.
TX740.D466 1998
641.8'12--dc21
                                98-4414
                                CIP

ISBN: 0-609-60151-2

10 9 8 7 6 5 4 3 2 1

First American Edition

CONTENTS

SOUTHERN ITALY.

PAPAL

STATES

GULF OF VENICE

THE CARNIVAL

STRAIT OF BONIFACIO

BENEVENTO.

NAPLES AND VESUVIUS.

ÆOLIAN
LIPARI ISLANDS

GULF OF TARANTO

FESTIVAL OF THE VINTAGE.

SCALE

M E D I T E R R A N E A N

A F R I C A

TUNIS

Longitude East from Greenwich

FOREWORD

EVERYDAY DURING MY COOKING CLASSES AT BADIA A COLTIBUONO WE TAKE A NOON break to enjoy a glass of white wine with an antipasto. It is always something simple and light, maybe a little toast topped with fresh, seasoned tomatoes or some deep-fried sage leaves. I take this opportunity to explain that antipasto does not mean something you eat before the pasta, as it is often mistranslated, but rather something you eat before the meal, pasto in Italian. I feel this is a useful clarification. By definition antipasti are additional to the menu. They stand outside the meal, as the French, hors d'oeuvre, rightly expresses it.

This means antipasti can be enjoyed in a variety of situations. You might serve them as an appetizer, before going to table, out in the garden or in the living room, while your guests are gathering and you are making the last preparations in the kitchen. Others are perfect on their own as a single course for a light luncheon or supper. Some are suitable substitutes for a more traditional and heavier first course of pasta or rice, to serve before the main course. Then, of course, there will be those occasions when you will want to enjoy the antipasto at table as the starter for a more traditional, several course meal. And what could be better for a midday or midnight snack than a bruschetta, a classic antipasto?

For this book I have selected recipes in keeping with this 'liberated' notion of antipasto, freed from any kind of formal structure. It would be a pity to confine the vast and rich repertoire of Italian antipasti dishes to those limited occasions when you might want to serve one of them as the so-called starter course of a meal.

I also hope these recipes will inspire you to welcome your guests, in whatever situation, with a really tasty dish to begin the occasion. Can anything be more unappetizing than being offered some of those miserable little packaged things that are often served? The meal that follows could be quite wonderful but unfortunately first impressions last. On the other hand when I see guests eat my antipasto offering, be it simple or sophisticated, with a certain relish, I know they understand that I have taken care to provide for their pleasure. Whenever we entertain, be it a cocktail party, buffet, banquet, informal luncheon, formal dinner or light supper, we should commence with our best efforts.

Notwithstanding centuries of tradition, antipasti are also among the most contemporary offerings of the Italian table. They are mostly light, easy to prepare, flexible and attractive to serve, and often an economic way to entertain a large number of guests. As you will see and hopefully taste for yourselves, some of the most interesting and delicious dishes in Italian culinary tradition are found among the antipasti. The range is extraordinary, incorporating every food and flavour from raw vegetables, fish and meat to preparations with complex, savoury sauces. In these recipes you will find over 200 tasty dishes to satisfy your guests on the spot or to stimulate their appetites and expectations for what is to come.

The Story of Antipasti

As far back as recorded history takes us, at least with regard to eating habits on the Italian peninsula, credit goes to the ancient Romans for first coming up with the intelligent and happy custom of stimulating the appetite with savory and often times sweet dishes before settling down to the main meal. The roots of this gastronomic tradition sprang, like many creative innovations in cultural evolution, from two contrasting sources, wealth with the leisure it brings, and necessity, 'the mother of invention'. Put in another way, antipasti had their beginnings both as banquet fare and as street food.

Plenty of evidence exists in the historical accounts of the extravagant banquets of the Roman leisured classes to see how the antipasto course, as we would come to know it in later times, took shape. No real recipes have survived from these eating orgies — it would seem the diners were lucky if they even survived. What we do know something about is the sheer number and type of dishes that the Romans served to bring on an appetite before the more serious courses — the bears, bulls, peacocks, flamingos and what have you — were brought on.

In Latin these dishes were described as the *gustationes* (tastings), or the *antecoena* (a word which means practically the same thing as the Italian antipasto). The satirical poet, Juvenal, portrays the Roman general Lucullus, of the famous *"Lucullan"* feasts, stretched out on his couch, eyeing the vast variety of *gustationes* making the rounds of the banquet table, as well as the comely slaves who were serving them, and selecting so many *gustationes* that before the meal had even commenced he had *"eaten up a whole estate"*. Perhaps the difficulty of digestion while reclining on a banqueting coach for lengthy periods of time might also have had something to do with the preference for tasting a little bit from a lot of dishes.

A description by Petronius in the *Satyricon* of one of the notorious feasts given by Trimalchius, who seems to have been the most degenerate of the Roman gourmands, gives us some idea of the kind of dishes that were served as *gustationes*. Among many others he mentions pork sausages, honey cakes, soft cheeses, "a snail for each person", tripe, stuffed eggs, ham and olives cured in brine. Apart from the honey cakes, all

these dishes can still be found today on the antipasto table of almost any traditional Roman restaurant.

The Roman gastronome, Apicius, in his account of the cooking and eating habits of Imperial Rome, *De Re Coquinaria* (Concerning Culinary Matters), mentions other food combinations that are popular as antipasto even to this day. For example, *prosciutto* with figs, and eel marinated in a sweet-and-sour sauce. Whereas his renowned recipe for dormouse cooked in honey and rolled in poppy seeds has most definitely gone out of date.

In a letter from the author of the *Epigrams*, Martial, we get a good idea of a more typically middle-class menu in first-century Rome. He writes of *"a modest dinner"* he is planning for about seven guests, that *"shall consist of a single course"* featuring several different dishes, kid, meat balls, chicken and ham, accompanied by beans and sprouts, and preceded by an antipasto of mallows, lettuces, leeks, sliced eggs, fresh fish and tripe "dripping with tuna brine". The supper concludes with fresh apples, aged wine and *"jests without gall"*.

In antipasti not only have we inherited some of the substance of ancient Roman banquets but also something of their spirit. I am referring to the Roman ability to make any meal a festive occasion. This is nowhere more apparent than when you walk into a traditional restaurant in Rome and are greeted by a lavish and colourful array of antipasti dishes, usually strategically placed near the entrance door or in the centre of the dining room, so that all who enter will be subject to its enticements. Immediately these antipasti create a festive mood, even if your intention was simply to sit down and have a little lunch.

Il ritorno alle allegre tradizioni locali. A Guastalla è stata ristabilita, dopo dodici anni, la curiosissima "Festa degli gnocchi,,. Prima di essere distribuiti al popolo, — che quest'anno ne ha ricevuti dieci quintali — gli gnocchi vengono assaggiati dal re della festa, che è scelto fra i più cospicui mangiatori della città. (Disegno di A. Beltrame).

Il "crescione,, = pianta che si consuma cruda e anche cotta = richiede acqua di sorgente la quale
gela con minore facilità

Meanwhile, back in ancient Rome, as the emperor and his cohorts were engaging in their riotous feasting, the silent majority outside the palace walls were making do with the little they had using the large amount of ingenuity that seems to have always been a characteristic of the Italian home cook.

Written, as well as archaeological, testimony tell us something about the eating habits of the Roman *plebs*. From the ruins of Pompeii outside of Naples, which was a Greek and then a Roman city, and the remains of markets like Trajan's in the city of Rome, it is evident that the common folk liked to snack when they shopped and socialized. The writer, Cato, who was also a statesman and spent a lot of time in the Forum which adjoined Trajan's market, mentions enjoying *torta scriblita*, a little sheep's cheese tart, which was sold by vendors in the market. In his time these tarts were street food. Today they live on as *scrippelle*, a pancake (crêpe) filled with *pecorino* cheese, still a speciality of the Abruzzi, where they are served as an antipasto or in broth as a first course. Cicero, the Roman orator who often held forth in the neighbouring Forum, was fond of little chick-pea pancakes. From his description these sound similar to the *farinata* of Liguria, a thick pancake (crêpe) made with chick-pea flour. *Farinate* are still made by vendors in Genova and eaten on the street, washed down with a glass of white wine, before going home for dinner.

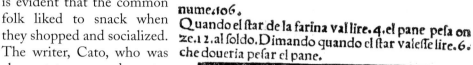

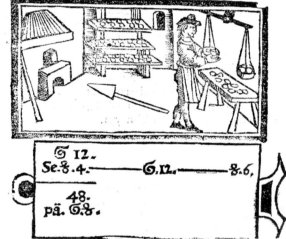

From contemporary carvings that decorate the streets of Pompeii as well as Trajan's market, we can see that besides butcher shops and bakeries there were also stalls that roasted and fried food, ready to eat on the spot or to take home. Most houses had no kitchen, so this was a necessity as well as a convenience.

When I first visited Rome after the war this kind of street food was still available, especially in the older neighbourhoods. You could buy *suppli'*, plump rice balls filled with mozzarella or *provola* cheese and fried to a golden brown. My Roman girlfriends called these *suppli' al telefono*, telephone croquettes, because the cheese was stringy like telephone wires and tended to get tangled up on our faces and fingers when we ate them. Today the demands of modern life have all but eliminated street food. Now you are most likely to be served a *suppli'* as an antipasto, brought to the table while you are deciding what to order for lunch.

It is difficult to get an idea of how antipasti fared in the Italy of the late Middle Ages. From the very few menus that have survived the period, it appears most festive meals in aristocratic families began with a fruit course, to stimulate the digestive juices. Manuscripts mention *entremets* or *piatti di mezzo*, served between the several main courses. They were composed of dishes that today we would consider antipasti: stuffed eggs and omelets, fish and meat in gelatine, deep-fried vegetables and cheese. In a cookery book written by an anonymous Tuscan in the late Middle Ages, several references are made to *crespelle*, stuffed pancakes (crêpes). *Crespelle alla fiorentina*, filled with spinach and sheep's milk ricotta and covered with *béchamel* make an elegant dish that you might expect to be served as an antipasto in a Florentine home today.

In fifteenth-century Renaissance Italy, when Italians were rediscovering their classic cultural heritage, a rebirth of culinary arts, inspired by ancient Rome, also took place. During this period a formal meal began with a series of hot and cold dishes, seasoned with both sweet and savoury sauces and served on a sideboard. These were known as *servizio di credenza*. The dishes were attractively displayed on the *credenza* and served from there. (Dozens of the raised engraved silver platters on which these were served can be seen in the splendid Medici collection in Palazzo Pitti in Florence.) At the same meal another series of dishes, this time hot, would be served from the kitchen. These were called *servizio di cucina* and they alternated with the cold dishes.

We are able to get an idea of the range of these dishes thanks to Bartolomeo Scappi, personal cook to several cardinals and to one pope during the mid-sixteenth century. He was a prolific writer and left for posterity a six-volume cookery book, now referred to as his *Opera*, his life 'Works'. He records over a hundred menus listing at least a thousand dishes.

On October 28, the feast of San Fiorenzo, Scappi orchestrated a six-course banquet, each course consisting of dozens of dishes, beginning with twenty-four antipasti and ending with twenty-one *postpasti*, or desserts. In between, the four main courses were served.

To give you just a taste of a Renaissance meal, the following typical mixture of sweet and savoury dishes were included in the *servizio di credenza* or antipasto course. The banquet begins with several sweet dishes, such as *offelle*, sweet pastries and marzipan cookies and meringues. These were followed by little caviar toasts topped with a bitter orange sauce; *bottarga*, fish roe cut into strips and dressed with olive oil, vinegar and pepper; *Galli d'India*, slices of roast turkey with little clams and seasoned with sugar; grilled herring salad; sliced sausages cooked in red wine; salted eel; calf's foot aspic on a bed of very finely chopped capon; *carpione*, fish marinated in a sweet-and-sour sauce; slices of ham baked in wine; pickled ox tongue, and fresh anchovies dressed with olive oil, vinegar and oregano. Apart from the sweets, all these dishes can still be found on the traditional antipasto table. In most cases only the seasoning and dressing have changed.

By the early seventeenth century the salad as an antipasto seems to have come into its own. Lettuce had been mentioned in ancient Roman documents as a *gustatio* to begin a meal, but no indication was given as to how it was eaten. Now we learn what constituted a proper salad and how it was dressed. In 1627, Salvatore Massoio dedicated an entire treatise to salad. As an antipasto he highly recommends a salad "*da irritamento*", to "irritate" or provoke the appetite. It

should be composed of herbs and the quantity, he writes, should be enough only to stimulate, not satiate the appetite.

Massoio does not give a recipe for his salad, as he takes for granted that any Italian worth his salt would know how to compose one. However, another writer of the same period, Giacomo Castelvetro, in exile in England, felt he could not trust "the Germans and other uncouth nations, especially the English who are even worse" to make and dress a decent salad, so he sets out to teach them in his marvellous little book, *The Fruit, Herbs and Vegetables of Italy*. Before giving instructions on how to wash the leaves for a salad, he reminds his readers that "*first you must wash your hands*".

Castelvetro's recipe for a mixed salad, "*the best and most wonderful of all*" consists of young mint leaves, garden cress, basil, lemon balm, tips of salad burnet, tarragon, borage leaves and flowers, fennel, rocket (arugula), sorrel, rosemary flowers, a few sweet violets and just the hearts of lettuce. Several years ago I began making almost this exact same salad, varying with the season, for one of the cooking class luncheons, not realizing at the time that I was transmitting a centuries-old tradition.

As a dressing for the mixed salad he recommends plenty of salt, a generous amount of oil and just a little vinegar – not like the English, whom he says use enough vinegar for a footbath. Italians now eat salad after the main course, subscribing to the theory that it aids digestion. When I first went to the United States years ago, I remember finding it strange that the salad was served before the main course, an antipasto of sorts, as recommended by Castelvetro in the seventeenth century.

It is interesting to note that Castelvetro mentions another Italian salad made not only with a profusion of greens but also raisins, olives, capers, ox tongue, candied citron, lemon peel and spring onion. Composed salads of this kind are again becoming popular in Italy as an antipasto or as the main course of a luncheon.

The best picture of Italian eating habits in the nineteenth century can be gathered from Pelligrino

Artusi's celebrated book, *La Scienza in cucina e l'Arte di mangiar bene* (The Science of Cooking and the Art of Eating Well), a best-seller for over one hundred years. As its subtitle states, it is "a practical manual for families", and generations of homecooks have known it simply and affectionately as *"Artusi"*.

In Artusi's time, the formal family meal of the *bourgeoisie* class he had in mind as readers consisted of six or seven courses, and often more than one dish was served for each course. He refers to antipasti as *principii*, 'starters', and puts them after the recipe sections for first courses, soups, pasta and rice. In the introduction he says that *principii* can be served either before or after the first course, but he prefers to follow "the Tuscan custom" of eating it after, which he considers "more reasonable".

The actual selection of antipasto recipes may seem somewhat disappointing. There are only ten entries and eight of them are for *crostini*, with capers, truffles, chicken liver, anchovies, and the most interesting one, with woodcock. Of the other two, one is for what he

calls "sandwiches", with either ham or tongue, and the other, for *baccala montebianco*, salt cod whipped with cream to resemble a snow-covered mountain, which seems an odd choice. Artusi himself found this a bizarre name for the recipe, suggesting as it does the famous chestnut purée and whipped cream dessert, although he says it makes a delicious antipasto.

What can be deduced from Artusi is that antipasti were not a standard part of a family meal. The *trasmesso* course, sometimes called *piatti di mezzo*, or the course served in-between the main courses, was more important. Many of his recipes for *piatti di mezzo* are served today as antipasti, stuffed vegetables, little *pizze*, moulded dishes, dressed eggs and omelets.

Ada Boni, the most important cookery writer of the first half of the twentieth century, in her charmingly entitled *Il Talismano della Felicità*, (The Charm of Felicity) dedicates more than thirty pages to antipasto, an exhaustive treatment. In the introduction she states that the recipes contained in the sections on *intermezzi*, *entremets,* fried foods and salads, are also suitable for the antipasto course.

This brings us to the present. Today the antipasto course has gone through some essential changes not in substance but in style, having to do with when and how it is served. These changes reflect a shift in contemporary attitudes to health, diet, work and leisure-time schedules. With today's lifestyle who wants to sit down to a daily repast of several courses?

The classic repertoire of recipes is still prepared but often these dishes have changed their position on the menu. Dishes that were traditionally served as starters (appetizers) to a meal are now frequently served as a first course, in place of a heavier pasta dish, for instance. I may serve as the main course for a light supper a dish my mother would have put on the menu as an *entremets* between courses. I would merely increase the quantities. For a single-course summer luncheon I might go to the antipasto section of Ada Boni and select several of her recipes for *frittate,* and serve them along with a simple green salad. Artusi's *crostini,* which nineteenth-century hostesses incorporated into their dinner menus, I might offer my guests with an *aperitivo* glass of white wine, while we wait to go to the table.

Of course, there is a time for feasting and the antipasti of ancient Roman and Renaissance banquets still appear on contemporary buffet tables and in the antipasto offerings of fine traditional restaurants. For formal dinner parties I compose a menu consisting of several courses and will usually choose a delicious warm antipasto of fish or fowl to let my guests know they are in for a gastronomic treat that evening.

In short, glancing over more than 2000 years of Italian gastronomic history, I come to the happy conclusion that our rich culinary tradition of antipasti has not only survived intact, but it continues to thrive.

PART I

TYPES OF ANTIPASTI
&
THE ANTIPASTO PANTRY

TYPES OF ANTIPASTI

IN THE RECIPE CHAPTERS I HAVE ORGANIZED THE DISHES TO MAKE THEM EASILY ACCESSIBLE WHEN YOU WANT TO PLAN A MENU OR GET DOWN TO COOKING. IN THIS SECTION I DESCRIBE THE VAST AND RICH ARRAY OF DISHES THAT TRADITIONALLY COMPOSE THE CLASSIC ANTIPASTO COURSE OF THE ITALIAN MEAL, EVEN THOUGH MANY OF THEM YOU MAY NEVER HAVE OCCASION TO PREPARE. IMAGINE THAT WELL-LADEN TABLE WITH ITS DISPLAY OF DOZENS OF ANTIPASTI WHICH GREETS YOU AS YOU ENTER A TRADITIONAL EATING ESTABLISHMENT IN ANY ITALIAN TOWN. WHAT FOLLOWS SHOULD HELP YOU IDENTIFY THE OFTEN UNFAMILIAR FOOD ON ALL THOSE PLATTERS.

A hint for travellers. If you are an adventurous eater with an interest in the diversity of regional foods, I would recommend, when you are visiting any of the twenty different regions along the Italian peninsula, that you investigate their antipasto offerings. Often local cooks, in homes as well as in restaurants, will present their region's most unusual and interesting dishes as an antipasto.

For my purposes here, all traditional antipasti dishes can be divided into two categories, the *affettato*, comprised of sliced cured meats and the *antipasto misto*, mixed antipasti dishes, which I have further divided into four different kinds according to their basic ingredient, bread, vegetables, cheese and eggs and seafood.

SLICED CURED MEATS

Affettato

When you are seated at an Italian restaurant table as a guest at a celebration, perhaps nothing heralds more exuberantly the abundance of the feast to follow than those large platters of sliced cured meats brought to the table by a bevy of waiters in white jackets. This is probably the most classic antipasto in the Italian repertoire. The type of meat is usually pork, although it can sometimes be beef, and might include more exotic delicacies such as boar, goose, turkey, deer, goat and even horse or donkey.

Traditionally these sliced meats are served as antipasti in restaurants at the noon meal for banquets and other special occasions. At Sunday lunch in homes out in the country, especially if there are guests at the table, almost certainly the hosts will proudly offer meats they or one of their neighbours have cured themselves. At least one platter of *affettato* is usually found on a buffet table. And, of course, these meats often make up the main course of an informal lunch.

Since these meats must be professionally cured and no instruction is needed on how to serve them, I have not included them in the recipe section, except in combination with other ingredients. Here, however, I list the ones you are most likely to find on a traditional antipasto platter in a restaurant. This might also come in handy should you be on the road and shopping for a picnic. With a few slices of cured meats, perhaps some cheese, several freshly baked rolls, a handful of olives and a bottle of wine you will be set.

Culatello, a speciality from the northern region of Emilia, is considered the king of pork products. It is a piece of ham taken from the upper and outer part of the pig's thigh, that is, its posterior. *Culo*, in fact, is the rude word for buttocks and the *tello* at the end is an Italian diminutive form which could be translated in this context as cute little. The fillet is cut away from the bone and then massaged with a mixture of rock salt, ground black pepper, crushed garlic and a pinch of fresh nutmeg. Since it is a muscle that does not have the protective fat of *prosciutto*, it is sealed in pig's bladder,

BEEF

Hind Quarter	Fore Quarter
1 Sir Loin	10 Fore Rib... 5 Ribs
2 Rump	11 Middle D?.4 D?
3 Aitch Bone	12 Chuck... 3 D?
4 Buttock	13 Shol? or Leg Mutt? piece
5 Mouse D?	14 Brisket
6 Veiny piece	15 Clod
7 Thick Flank	16 Neck or Sticking piece
8 Thin D?	17 Shin
9 Leg	18 Cheek

before being hung to age in a damp cellar. The right degree of humidity is essential to the ageing process, as one of the most valued characteristics of *culatello* is its tenderness. The meat is pale pink with just a thin, milky marbling of fat and has a rich and mellow flavour.

The best *culatello* is reputed to come from the town of Zibello outside of Parma. When the genuine product is served as an antipasto, it is presented on its own, as befits royalty, never eaten with figs or melon. In its native region it is often accompanied by a kind of deep fried flat bread cut into diamond or square shapes called *crescente*, or in Parma *torta fritta*. If you are ever in the area, don't miss the opportunity to taste this supremely excellent antipasto.

If *culatello* is the king of cured pork products, *prosciutto*, the hind thigh of the pig, is the prince. One reason *culatello* is so rare and expensive is that to make it the butcher has to sacrifice the much larger and profitable *prosciutto*. The most renowned *prosciutto* comes from the countryside around Parma, "Parma ham", but *prosciutto* from the areas of San Daniele and Sauris in the region of Friuli is considered by many to be even superior. And in central Italy many farmers still raise a family pig and come winter make their own variety of *prosciutto* as well as other cured pork products.

Traditionally *prosciutto* is made from a year-old pig that has been raised on a special diet which, in the province of Parma, includes whey left over from the making of parmesan cheese. Excess fat is cut away from the thigh, producing its characteristic mandolin shape. Then it is put under salt for several weeks, before being hung to age for the better part of a year in rooms with controlled temperature and humidity.

Prosciutto is dark pink in colour with ribbons of fat, although today's *prosciutti* are leaner than in the past. Its degree

of saltiness varies. Hams from the north of Italy are sweeter, that is, less salty, while in central Italy the locals like theirs on the savoury side, the Tuscans in particular.

Prosciutto is usually sliced paper-thin using a machine, although some traditionalists prefer it thicker, cut with a knife. An antipasto platter of *prosciutto* will sometimes be garnished with curls of butter. It is often served with fruit – melons and figs form the classic combinations. For a buffet I sometimes wrap thin slices of *prosciutto* around the top of bread sticks, usually ones that have been rolled in fresh rosemary or poppy seeds before they were baked.

When you visit a *prosciutto*-producing area of Italy, be sure to try the local product. Beware, however. Today many "Italian" *prosciutti* come from pigs that were industrially and economically fattened over several months in Northern Europe and merely processed in Italy.

A relatively recent arrival on the antipasto table, at least nationwide, is *speck*, smoked *prosciutto*, an ancient tradition of the Alto Adige region of Italy, where it crossed over the border from Austria. It is now popular and can be found everywhere. I particularly like its smoked flavour and incorporate *speck* into many recipes. I often use it in place of bacon, as it is leaner.

Similar to *prosciutto* are two other less expensive (and many would say even more flavourful) cuts that are traditionally served as antipasti. *Coppa*, sometimes called *spalla*, is the pig's shoulder boned and rolled, cured in salt, seasoned with pepper and nutmeg and aged for several months. It is less tender than *prosciutto* but has a more earthy bite. *Capocollo* is a cut taken from the section between the head and shoulder and is richer in flavour than *prosciutto*. These are both

PORK

1 The Sperib	4 Fore Loin
2 Hand	5 Hind D?
3 Belly or Spring	6 Leg

served cut thinly, but not in transparent slices like *prosciutto*. Set aside for a moment concerns about cholesterol counts and instead enjoy a delicious speciality of most pork-producing regions in Italy, *lardo*. This is cut from the layer of fat on the pig's back right beneath the skin and cured like *prosciutto*. As an antipasto, paper-thin slices, white with a rosy hue, are served with hot, grilled (broiled) bread, into which the *lardo* melts just like butter. Definitely worth any dietary risk!

Salame, or salami in English, is the generic word for chopped pork meat that is cured and served sliced, as distinct from sausages which are served whole. The word derives from salt, the curing agent. Salami are *insaccato*, which means the chopped meat is stuffed into a sack, traditionally the inverted and thoroughly washed intestine of the pig. Every region has its own varieties of *insaccati*, varying in size from gigantic cylinders of *mortadella*, sometimes simply called *bologna* after its home town, that usually weigh about 12 kg/24 lb but can top the scales at 50 kg/110 lb, to the tiny, sausage-sized salami typical of southern Italy.

In addition to differences regarding the breed of pig, how it was raised and how the product was aged, other variations among salami are due to the way the meat is ground (coarse or fine), the proportion of fat to lean meat and the type and degree of seasoning.

Depending on the region, a classic antipasto platter of *affettato* will include several different salami. *Salame Milano*, Milanese salami, is made with very finely ground pork and fat, and white wine is added to the seasoning. *Salame Felino* from Parma pigs is the leanest and most delicately flavoured salami. *Salame Toscano* is a fat round salami, rich and red, studded with large eyes of fat and flavoured with garlic and whole peppercorns. Another delicious Tuscan salami is called *finocchiona*, made of coarse-grained meat and seasoned with fennel seeds. In southern Italy they often add crushed chilli pepper and garlic to their salami. One of the tastiest of all *insaccati* is *soppressata*, a large marbled salami similar to brawn and head cheese. The bits and pieces of the pig left over from processing other cuts are boiled together with the head, seasoned with spices and orange rind (peel) and pressed together to form a loaf. I don't know if anyone has ever tried to come up with an exhaustive list of Italian salami but they certainly number many dozens and are one of the great treasures and pleasures of regional gastronomy.

Travelling through Italy you will discover a few non-pork meats that are salt cured and served sliced as an antipasto. They are local in character and some are on the slightly exotic side; horse in the province of Mantova; wild boar in the province of Siena; wild goat,

mocetta, from the Valle d'Aosta, which is flavoured with juniper berries, and goose in the province of Pavia, a contribution from Jewish culture and cooking.

Bresaola, cured beef, a speciality of the Valtellina, a valley in the Alps of Lombardia, merits special mention, because it makes an especially delicious antipasto and deservedly has found favour throughout Italy. *Bresaola* is to beef what *prosciutto* is to pork. It is fillet of beef, salt cured, air dried and aged for several months. The flavour is sharper yet more delicate than *prosciutto*. *Bresaola* is often served dressed like *carpaccio*. You cover a platter with thin slices and dress them with olive oil, lemon and freshly ground black pepper. Or try topping it with shavings of Parmesan cheese, raw artichokes or celery.

In conclusion let me mention a delicacy from my home town, Milano, that you should try when you visit. It is *nervetti*, boiled calf's feet. The meat is cut into strips and seasoned with olive oil, vinegar and sweet onions and served as an antipasto. Remarkably delicious. Another travel hint. The best place to shop in Italy for these kinds of antipasto is at the local *salumeria*, in Tuscany called a *pizzicheria*. Here you will find every imaginable kind of salami as well as a wide variety of cheeses and many of the *antipasti misti*, dishes of mixed antipasti that I describe below. Not far from where I live in Milano, near the Piazza del Duomo, is a food lover's paradise, where some of the most attractive and lavish food shops of Europe are located. This is the realm of Peck, a food emporium comprising several different shops laden with every delicious food you can imagine – salami, cheeses, exquisitely prepared dishes, pasta, breads, desserts and wines. So lavish and splendid and of such high quality is the selection, that it is worth a visit just to browse and to enjoy the visual and sensual feast. It is virtually impossible, however, to resist the temptation to indulge in something to take away or to eat on the spot.

La battaglia degli obesi. Il torneo che annualmente riunisce a Cavour i pesi massimi del Piemonte si è concluso con una superba affermazione del signor Luigi Favero di Settimo Torinese il quale con i suoi 176 chili ha nettamente battuto ogni concorrente. Dopo la proclamazione del vincitore è seguito un pranzo di oltre cinque ore. Accanto al neo-"re dei grassoni", è la "reginetta", l'attrice Speranza Gorini di Torino. Un quintale e mezzo. (Disegno di Walter Molino)

1. *Shirley*

2. *Plum*

3. *Golden Sunrise*

4. *Grenadier*

5. *Ailsa Craig*

6. *Gardener's Delight*

7. *Mirabel*

8. *Dombello*

9. *Tigerella*

10. *Alicante*

11. *Liberto*

THE *only* WAY TO MAKE A TOMATO SALAD. FIRST, CUT OFF THE 'LIDS' FROM SOME MEDIUM SIZED TOMATOES THEN HOLLOW THEM OUT. SPRINKLE THE INSIDE WITH GREEN BEANS, MANGETOUT PEAS, SLICED CELERY AND COURGETTE PIECES WITH SOME *HELLMANN'S* MAYONNAISE AND USE TO FILL THE TOMATOES. GARNISH

BREAD–BASED ANTIPASTI

If a platter of sliced cured meats is the most traditional antipasto, those based on bread are the most primordial. From the very beginning of civilization on the Italian peninsula there would have been bread and something to eat with it or on it.

During the months of November and December, especially in Tuscany and other regions where high-quality olive oil is produced, *fettunta* is the favourite seasonal antipasto. The word means *"an oiled slice of bread"* and the dish really does not require much more explanation. To make it you simply cut a thick slice of country-style bread, grill (broil) it, preferably over charcoal, rub it with a clove of garlic while it is still hot, sprinkle it with a little salt and thoroughly douse it with new oil, *olio nuovo*. This is bright green and cloudy because it is unfiltered and has a peppery flavour. This is really just a way of tasting the new oil. The bread merely forms a base.

I prefer to reserve the Tuscan word *fettunta* for the annual, seasonal event when freshly pressed oil is available. Otherwise, *bruschetta*, the Roman word for grilled bread dressed with olive oil, is better used. The essential factor is that the olive oil be high- quality extra virgin. Recently I have noticed that a variation on this dish has become popular in restaurants outside of Italy. A little bowl of olive oil in which to dip bread is brought to the table instead of butter. Nothing wrong with this, as long as the olive oil is a high-quality extra virgin. If not, which has mostly been my experience, the usual patty of butter would be preferable. As an antipasto or even as a light lunch in themselves, *bruschetta* can be dressed with other seasonal ingredients – broad (fava) beans, fresh tomatoes, florets of cooked cauliflower, white beans, for example – all generously seasoned with

fresh, uncooked extra-virgin olive oil. You will find many of my favourite combinations in the recipe section.

Crostini are tiny slices of bread usually cut from a small round loaf called a *frusta* and spread with various mixtures, chicken liver pâté or various *burri composti,* butter mixed with other ingredients, traditionally anchovies, parsley or truffles. The bread for *crostini* must not be soft but crusty or toasted. With many spreads *crostini* are best if served while still warm.

A popular contemporary variation on this traditional theme are *crostoni*, large slices of bread topped with various ingredients. *Crostoni* can make a meal in themselves. Restaurants are beginning to feature them on the menu, almost like pizza. Recently a restaurant has opened in Florence that serves exclusively *crostoni*, at least a dozen varieties. It seems it is now more fashionable to call *bruschette*, *crostoni*, at least when they are served as a single course meal and not as an antipasto, but technically there is no difference between the two.

Instead of bread, little squares or wedges of fried polenta can also be eaten like *crostini*, topped with a dressing of mushrooms or tomatoes. These make a tasty warm antipasto for winter.

Several pizza-type dishes are often served as antipasti. Usually these are little *pizzette* and small rounds of flat bread called *focacce*, topped with one simple ingredient or a tasty combination. In restaurants on the Italian Riviera a dish called *pissaladiera* is often served as an antipasto. It is made with pizza dough and topped with a rich and savory dressing of onions, olives and anchovies, seasoned with olive oil. I have chosen some of my favourite recipes for these delicious *pizzette*, which are especially useful for serving as finger food at large cocktail parties and buffets.

VEGETABLE ANTIPASTI

In one form or another the lavish array of vegetables from the Italian garden from the tip to the toe of the peninsula are displayed on the traditional antipasto table of restaurants. Some are meant to be combined with other antipasti, others constitute a course by themselves. Of the later kind, I think the dish that best embodies this richness is the colourful, healthy and tasty *pinzimonio*. The word itself denotes a tangy flavour and refers to the condiment, olive oil seasoned with salt and pepper, into which you dip an assortment of thinly sliced, raw vegetables – fennel, artichokes, celery, radishes, Belgian chicory (endive), carrots and (bell) peppers are the most common. These are usually presented on a large platter set in the middle of the table. At the place of each guest you place a tiny ceramic bowl containing the olive oil and then everyone proceeds to dip and chomp.

The Romans claim they created this dish and certainly their region produces profuse and marvellous vegetables. To my taste, however, Tuscany has the most delicious olive oil, so the ideal marriage might be a combination of the two. *Pinzimonio* is a personal favourite of mine and I have included it in the recipe section (see page 82).

Similar in style to *pinzimonio*, though not in substance, is a classic vegetable antipasto from Piemonte called, in local dialect, *bagna cauda*, meaning "warm bath", that refers to its sauce made from lots of garlic, anchovy fillets, butter and olive oil. The sauce is kept hot in a terracotta pot over a candle or spirit lamp set in the middle of the table, fondue style, into which the diners dip raw and sometimes parboiled vegetables. The traditional raw vegetables for *bagna cauda* are artichokes, broccoli, spinach, (bell) peppers, celery, carrots, fennel and most typical of all, cardoons. In Piemonte parboiled onions and potatoes will also be on the platter.

Whereas *pinzimonio* is a dish best suited for spring and summer, *bagna cauda* is perfect for chilly autumn and winter evenings, eaten with lots of country bread and washed down with abundant new red wine. I spent many happy hours of my childhood in my grandmother's castle in Piemonte and have comforting memories of sharing *bagna cauda* with my cousins. At the end of the meal my grandmother would fry an egg for each of us in the remains of the sauce. *"Good for the digestion,"* she would remind us.

A term for a wide range of vegetable antipasti is *sottaceti*, which means preserved in vinegar. Cauliflower florets, carrots, mushrooms, onions and courgette (zucchini) are blanched, cut into pieces, placed in a jar with com-plementary seasonings, such as thyme, mint, salt and peppercorns, covered with high-quality white wine vinegar and sealed. Little platters of these vegetables are traditionally found on restaurant antipasti tables as well as at festive family gatherings. These titbits are prized for stimulating the appetite before a big meal. Purists will tell you they should not be eaten with the more delicately favoured cured meats, such as fine *prosciutto*. And vinegar, of course, tends to affect the taste of wine. Similar antipasti are vegetables *sottoli*, conserved in olive oil. These are traditionally produced in regions favoured with an abundance of olive oil. The better the quality of oil used the better the taste. I think little artichokes are among the best of these. Mushrooms and *asparagini*, wild asparagus, are also delicious.

Both *sottaceti* and *sottoli* can be preserved at home or bought commercially. In many regions small fine food companies produce high-quality products of this kind. In the section on basic recipes I have given instructions on how to make *sottaceti* and *sottoli*, so you will be able to preserve them yourselves and always have a supply on hand in the pantry.

Perhaps this is the best place to include the many varieties of Italian table olives. When all is said and done this fruit of the olive tree, whether black or green, stuffed or stoned, plain or packed with seasonings is certainly the most simple and often the most satisfying of all antipasto.

Every olive-producing region has its particular variety and recipe for curing and seasoning. Among the most notable are the extra-large, firm, green olives, eommonly from Calabria, which are salt-brine cured; the yellowish-green; soft olives from Sicilia that are often marinated in olive oil and chilli pepper; the shiny purple-black ones from Liguria; the little black wrinkled olives, often from central Italy, which have been brine cured and then dried briefly in an oven and *Gaeta* olives,

VENEZIA. – UN CAFFÈ IN RIVA DEGLI SCHIAVONI.

black, dry-salt cured and then rubbed with oil, the most popular olive for cooking, especially in the south. In a *salumerie* you will find a baffling choice but Italian shopkeepers are normally very helpful and happy to let you taste before you choose.

A remarkable antipasto you can order in most classic restaurants from Rome to Napoli is *fritto misto vegetariano*, mixed vegetable fry, to distinguish it from a mixed deep fry that includes bits of meat. It consists of a variety of greens and vegetables covered with a very light batter and deep fried with an even lighter touch by an expert chef. On the platter you could expect to find deep-fried courgette (zucchini)-flowers, globe artichokes, a speciality of the Jewish quarter in Rome, aubergines (eggplants), asparagus tips, onions, (bell) peppers, fennel, cauliflower florets and porcini mushroom caps. In most restaurants a *fritto misto vegetariano* will also include little balls of deep-fried mozzarella cheese.

Each season provides its own additions to the vegetable platters on the antipasto table. In spring I look forward to white asparagus. The best come from the region of Friuli on the north eastern border with Austria. The spears are steamed, dressed simply with olive oil and lemon juice and served at room temperature.

Another vegetable that marks the arrival of spring in the markets and on the antipasto table are broad (fava) beans, favourite appetite teasers. If you were to walk through the back streets of the Trastevere area in Rome on May Day, you would come across men sitting outside playing cards and eating broad beans straight from their shells, maybe with a chuck of piquant *pecorino romano*, local sheep's milk cheese. The combination brings on not only an appetite but a thirst that is quenched with deep quaffs of white wine from the Frascati hills. In Tuscany raw broad beans are sometimes served at the end of the meal. As an antipasto they are combined with diced pieces of sweet *pecorino toscano* and dressed with olive oil.

The tomato, one of the summer glories of the Italian garden, appears on the antipasto table in various dress, most often cut in half, sprinkled with parsley and garlic, browned in the oven and filled with various ingredients. Best of all, in southern Italy bowls of tiny vine-ripened tomatoes called *pomodorini* are set before you. These are so intense in flavour they can be eaten like candy, popped into the mouth just as they are.

Sun-dried tomatoes are another typical Southern antipasto of the *sottolio* type. The tomatoes are cut in half, salted and put out into the sun to dry for a few days. They are then preserved with olive oil to which seasonings such as oregano and garlic might be added. When properly preserved using a good tomato and high-quality oil these can be delicious eaten on their own, or as a garnish with other antipasti.

Another very popular vegetable appetizer you will often see displayed in *salumerie* is a dish that might not seem very Italian and in fact is called *insalata russa*, Russian salad. It is made of assorted diced vegetables, beetroots, potatoes, carrots, green beans and peas – about as many vegetables as ethnic races in Russia – bound together by a rich olive-oil mayonnaise. It is always handsomely presented and colourfully garnished on a large platter from which you can buy any size portion you wish.

In late summer and early autumn as (bell) peppers reach maturity they stand out as the most strikingly colourful vegetable on the antipasto table, reds, yellows and orange. These sweet peppers, roasted, cut into strips and marinated in olive oil with garlic cloves and maybe a little anchovy are delicious served as a topping for *bruschetta*. Roasted peppers stuffed with a variety of ingredients such as sheep's milk cheese, parsley, pine nuts and breadcrumbs, and served at room temperature, are another popular late summer, early autumn antipasto.

Next to the platter of peppers on the table there is likely to be a dish of roasted *melanzane* – aubergine (eggplant) – marinated in olive oil and flavoured with mint. In Sicilia look for *caponata*, slices of fried aubergine in a sweet-and-sour sauce of tomatoes, onions, capers and vinegar.

When autumn is at its fullness, if the weather has been warm and humid, wild mushrooms start popping up in the woods and most Italian country folk become, once again, foragers. They are searching above all for meaty, reddish-brown *porcini*, the *boletus*, and with a little luck if they know the special spots they might come home with a few exquisite *ovoli*, egg-mushrooms, so called because of the shape and colour of their cap before it opens. As antipasto, these and other mushrooms are mostly served raw and sliced in a salad, often combined with shavings of fresh Parmesan cheese and dressed with olive oil and lemon. The caps of cultivated mushrooms are prepared with a stuffing that includes dried wild *porcini* which lend an earthy, woody taste to these blander domestic varieties.

CHEESE AND EGGS

By itself cheese is not often eaten in Italy as a starter (appetizer). The great and notable exception is fresh buffalo mozzarella. When you are travelling in the several areas of southern Italy where water buffalo are raised, Battipaglia and Caserta in the region of Campania are the most celebrated, try an appetizer of *bocconcini*, little mouth-sized rounds of mozzarella, also called buffalo eggs. When they are really fresh they still release some of their buttermilk when you bite into them. In the South they say mozzarella should be eaten before noon on the day when it is made – a rare treat possible only when you are on the spot. In reputable establishments in other parts of Italy, it is worth trying the mozzarella. Even though it will be at least a day old, it will be fresher and superior to any you can possibly find outside of the country, even when it has been exported by air. Another cheese that has recently become a popular antipasto is *caprino*, goats' cheese. Formerly you had to be in certain areas of Sardegna, the Abruzzi or Calabria to taste *caprino*. Nowadays it is widely available. It usually comes in small, thick rounds that have been conserved in olive oil and herbs. In my native Milano they sell a cows' milk cheese which they call *caprino* because it comes in the same shape.

The only unique way Italians have of preparing the egg is in a *frittata*, which can loosely be described as an omelet, although it is unlike the French type in almost all respects. A *frittata* is round and flat. The eggs are cooked on the hob (top of the stove) very slowly until they are set but still soft in the centre and it is not folded over. One or a combination of other ingredients are usually added, cheese, onions, courgettes (zucchini) and mushrooms. Slices of *frittata* served at room temperature often form part of an antipasto course, especially on a buffet table. Italians also make use of the simple hard-cooked egg, variously stuffed or topped with a savoury green sauce.

SEAFOOD

The shape of the Italian peninsula is often described as a boot. Using that image, it must certainly be a fisherman's wader, immersed in the Mediterranean sea, which surrounds it on three sides. In fact, if you include the major islands of Sicilia and Sardinia as well as its numerous smaller ones, Italy has over 5000km/3000 miles of coastline. Fifteen of its twenty regions have seashores, and the other inland five have lakes and rivers. As a result seafood has always been easily available to the Italian cook and over the centuries a rich heritage of seafood as well as freshwater fish recipes have been developed nationwide.

Many of the best of these dishes are presented on the antipasto table and not just at the sea shore. Some of the cosmopolitan northern cities, such as Milano in the region of Lombardia which has no access to the sea, have the best fish in Italy. Remember that many Mediterranean species of fish are not found in other waters, so to taste many of these dishes you will have to come see for yourselves.

When I enter a good restaurant in Rome that specializes in fish, not a new-wave type of place but a traditional establishment, I am always amazed by the buckets, sometimes literally, of molluscs or shellfish. It reminds me that notwithstanding the overload of easily available packaged and frozen supermarket food, something of the forager or food gatherer remains in the human spirit, at least in the heart of a few fishermen from Lazio. Some of these molluscs are so minuscule, barely 3cm/1 ¼in, they hardly contain anything edible. There is a whole series of single-shell creatures called by various names, often with *chiocciola*, meaning snail, which they resemble, in their title. I remember when these were eaten raw but today one has to be more careful. Now they are usually boiled, maybe with a bay leaf to give additional flavour. You need a toothpick to pick them out of their shells.

On any worthy seafood antipasto table there will be numerous double-shelled molluscs. The most common are *cozze*, of the mussel family. In traditional fish restaurants platters of these are brought to the table steamed in white wine. Often they are served in the half shell, oven-browned with breadcrumbs, parsley, garlic and tomato. Three delicious molluscs are *datteri di mare*, date-shells; the rarer *tartufi di mare*, sea truffles, which are related to the more common *vongole* of the clam family, which come in all sizes; and the distinctive *cannolicchi* or razor clams. These are all esteemed antipasti.

Italy also has its own oysters, *ostriche*, which are now farmed in several northern and southern regions. I know many consider it a mistake, even a fault, to eat these expensive delicacies in any way other than raw with a squeeze of lemon but when you visit Puglia try

them baked with olive oil, breadcrumbs and parsley.

Seafood of the crustacean family – prawns, shrimp, lobster and crab – are more commonly prepared as a first course, in pasta sauces, risotto and soup, or as the main dish. The smaller varieties, however, *scampi* or *gamberetti*, little shrimp, are a classic antipasto, briefly simmered and simply dressed in olive oil and lemon juice. At Da Antonio, one of the best fish restaurants in all of Italy, surprisingly and happily located in Castelnuovo Berardenga in the centre of land-locked Chianti, one of Antonio's most delicious antipasto dishes is a large, single prawn. He peels away the shell from the tail, dresses it in a courgette (zucchini) blossom, in such a way that when you pull the tail away, you get a delicious mouthful of courgette (zucchini) blossom stuffed with the meaty tail of a tasty prawn.

One of the most appetizing seafood starts to any meal is a plate of *alici,* fresh anchovies. (The word *acciughe* usually refers to dried anchovies.) You used to see piles of fresh anchovies in Italian fish markets, their silvery scales glittering on the counter but they are now more scarce and industrial canners need to import them from Turkey and the Black Sea. Unfortunately they were over-fished in Italian waters. Even worse, they were dynamited from the bottom, so sadly their natural environment has been destroyed, probably irrevocably. However, small quantities of local fresh anchovies can still be had. They are best raw, filleted, opened up and marinated in olive oil and lemon juice. On the southern sea coasts cooks season them with chopped garlic, parsley, pepper and oregano. The taste of a very fresh anchovy is unique, so the less you do to it the better.

Romans, in particular, are fond of chunks of fine tuna preserved in olive oil as an antipasto. In Tuscany tuna is prepared with red onions and white beans. A simple yet more elegant presentation are tomatoes stuffed with tuna. Italians often buy the best-quality tuna, *ventresca*, tuna fish belly, at their local *salumeria*. It is sold by weight and taken from a large tin where it has been packed in olive oil.

A classic and delicious fish antipasto originated not in any of the coastal regions but in the Italian lake districts. It is an ancient dish variously named but most widely called *carpione*. Originally it was prepared with eel. Today sardines or other small fish are used.

These are lightly fried then marinated for several days in red wine vinegar seasoned with onion and bay. Venetians use the same treatment and add raisons and candied lemon rind (peel) to the marinade. They call the dish *saor*. In southern Italy mint is used to flavour the vinegar and they call the method *in scapece*.

In Lombardia on the Lago di Como they cure a local fish called *agone* in a different way. The fish is air dried and stored in special barrels before it is used to prepare a dish called in the local dialect, *missoltit*. The dried fish is first gently fried or grilled (broiled) until the skin comes away and then it is sprinkled with salt and red wine vinegar. At restaurants along the lake *missoltit* is served as an antipasto or as a main course with polenta.

In Italian restaurants that pride themselves on serving an international cuisine, smoked salmon and caviar are often on the menu as antipasti. You might, however, be better advised to try their more traditional and local offerings. The salmon will almost certainly be farmed, usually from Norway, although I have seen packaged smoked salmon from Ireland and even Canada in my village food shop. I can remember when you used to be able to find Italian caviar, *caviale*, from Po river sturgeon, but I can't remember the last time I saw it. For those who have wild smoked salmon and fine quality caviar available, I have included a couple of recipes that use both these delicious delicacies.

As the final entry on this list, I conclude with a food that is neither fish nor fowl. *Lumache*, snails, are a traditional antipasto in many parts of Italy, especially for special feast days and *feste*. Each region has its particular way of preparing these tricky but tasty creatures, which have to be put through an endless process of purgation and ablution before they are fit to eat. In Napoli, up until the middle of this century, snails were sold by vendors as a street snack, eaten on a piece of bread with a squeeze of lemon. In Piemonte snails are eaten coated in flour and fried in oil. Romans cook them in their shells with tomatoes onion, garlic and chili pepper. In a small town below our Tuscan home they hold an annual gastronomic feast in honour of the snail, *Sagra delle Lumache*. The featured starter is, of course, snails served in a thick tomato and *prosciutto* sauce. Forty per person is considered sufficient to get your appetite going.

THE ANTIPASTO PANTRY

THESE ARE SOME OF THE INDISPENSABLE PROVISIONS TO KEEP IN YOUR PANTRY, NOT ONLY FOR PREPARING ANTIPASTI BUT FOR NUMEROUS OTHER ITALIAN DISHES AS WELL. A SMALL SUPPLY OF THESE ESSENTIALS IS ESPECIALLY HANDY FOR IMPROMPTU ENTERTAINING.

ANCHOVIES

Try to find whole anchovy fillets packed in salt or ones that are preserved in olive oil and packed in jars, so you can see what you are getting. The meatiest ones are the best. The ones in jars can be used a few at a time and the rest kept in the refrigerater for up to several weeks. Do not use the packing oil as it is almost always low grade. Remember to rinse the salted ones well before using.

BREADCRUMBS

Use good stale bread and a blender or food processor to make dry breadcrumbs. They can be stored in a sealed glass jar, not in the refrigerator, and must be very dry when you use them. Perfectly adequate Italian brand packaged breadcrumbs are available. Avoid the "seasoned" variety.

BURRI COMPOSTI

Butter can be mixed with various savoury ingredients to a creamy consistency and used as a spread for *crostini* and *tartine*. Anchovy, *prosciutto*, parsley and truffle butters are easy to make at home using a food processor and they keep for several weeks in the refrigerator. Commercial truffle butters, especially those made with white truffles, vary greatly in quality. Look for *tuber magnatum pico* listed on the label. That is the name of *the* white truffle. You should also be able to detect through the jar little yellowish-brown truffle pieces in the butter itself.

CAPERS

The best capers in the world come from two small islands off the coast of Sicilia –

Pantelleria and Salina. Sicilian capers are usually preserved in salt, which is preferable to vinegar, as it does not alter their taste. Capers come in several sizes. I prefer the medium, which are more flavourful than the small ones and are more compact than the large. In Italy we can buy salted capers by weight. If you buy them in jars, pick the smallest quantity available, as they tend to dry out if kept for long periods even in the refrigerator. Rinse very well before using.

CHEESE

Parmigiano Reggiano is the finest of all Italian grating cheeses. Like extra virgin olive oil it is expensive but well worth the investment. Never buy grated parmesan in packets. A chunk of *Parmigiano* tightly wrapped first in cheese paper then in foil will keep for months in the refrigerator. The best *Parmigiano* is also an excellent table cheese.

FLOUR

For recipes calling for bread, pasta and pizza dough in Italy we use grade 0 or 00 flour. Unbleached plain (all-purpose) flour is a good substitute. Only recently has flour especially for making bread been packaged and sold in Italy.

GARLIC

Buy firm heads of garlic and store in a cool, dry place but not in the refrigerator. Garlic will keep for several weeks. Never substitute with dried or powdered garlic. Old garlic will form a green sprout which should be removed before the clove is used.

HERBS

Certain herbs are essential for Italian dishes. They are always better fresh but some may be substituted with the dried, but not the powdered, variety.

Basil does not dry well but it is easy to grow on a sunny windowsill. There are various ways of trying to preserve basil all year around. I have tried them all and have come to the conclusion that it is better to do without in winter and enjoy fresh basil when the warm seasons return.

Bay leaves, or *alloro*, Italian bay, are less pungent than the Pacific variety and have a very distinctive flavour. They are available dry from Italian grocery stores.

Marjoram, the wild Mediterranean variety, has a stronger flavour than cultivated sweet marjoram. It dries well.

Oregano is similar but stronger than marjoram and also dries well.

Parsley, the flat-leaf Italian variety has a definite flavour of its own and is what should be used for Italian dishes. It loses all of its flavour when dried but may instead be frozen.

Rosemary is a very popular Italian herb that retains its flavour when dried but not for more than for a few months.

Saffron is expensive because it is the tiny stamen of the crocus flower. Only use the best because inferior products are either flavourless or are mixed with turmeric and will make your dish taste like curry.

Sage has a strong, musty flavour. It dries fairly well.

MUSHROOMS

Dried *porcini* mushrooms are one of the most flavourful ingredients available for the pantry. The drying process cocentrates their wild and earthy taste. Choose packets containing large, cream coloured slices. Avoid ones that are dark and brittle looking. They keep indefinitely in a jar stored in a dry place and make a useful investment to bring back from a trip to Italy.

OLIVE OIL

Buy cold-pressed extra virgin olive oil. Nothing else will give an authentic flavour to your dish, and anything less will spoil the taste of the other ingredients. It is expensive to produce, so it is also expensive to buy. Be suspicious of bargains. Unfortunately, Italian labelling laws are confusing, so you need to find a reliable and knowledgeable shop keeper.

OLIVES

Always buy olives loose. A lot of their flavour is lost when black and green olives are stoned and canned.

ONIONS

Always have a few red and yellow onions with smooth and dry skins on hand. They will keep for weeks stored in a dark, dry place. When they sprout it is a sign they are beginning to rot inside.

PANCETTA

This is Italian unsmoked bacon, cured with salt and spices. If necessary, smoked bacon can be used as an alternative. You can hang a small slab of pancetta in a cool, well ventilated place or keep it wrapped up in the refrigerator.

PINE NUTS

Pinoli are the seeds of the Stone pine. In Italy they are packaged fresh, not toasted. Keep a small amount in store, as they are often called for in Italian recipes.

SPICES

Cloves should be used whole. Buy nutmeg whole and grate straight into the pan or dish. Black and white peppercorns should be ground as they are required. Use crushed dry *peperoncini*, or hot chilli pepper flakes.

TOMATOES

Every Italian pantry should have at least several jars of good Italian tomato sauce and cans of peeled whole plum tomatoes and tomato pulp. Tomato purée (paste) in tubes is a concentrate that can be added to canned sauce to increase flavour and consistency.

Sun-dried tomatoes should be bought preserved in olive oil, otherwise you will have to go through the process of reconstituting them and storing them in olive oil yourself.

TUNA

Invest in several cans of imported Italian tuna labelled *ventresca*, which comes from the belly of the fish, and is superior in taste and texture. It is packed in olive oil.

VINEGAR

Keep a couple of bottles of good-quality white and red wine vinegar on hand for sweet-and-sour sauces, for marinating meat and fish, and for preserving. You can also make your own aromatic vinegars by marinating various herbs in vinegar for several weeks and staining them afterwards. Tarragon, sage and basil work well and are useful for seasoning many dishes.

Balsamic Vinegar is an essential in the Italian pantry. The nomenclature and labelling regarding balsamic vinegar is confusing. First of all, authentic balsamic is not a vinegar but a condiment. It is produced in the provinces of Modena and Reggio in the region of Emilia-Romagna and made from the boiled-down must of sweet white Trebbiano grapes. It is then aged for decades in a battery of casks of varying sizes made of different woods. This condiment has a deep, luminous brown colour, a consistency that is dense and syrupy, a complex, intense aroma that is pleasantly acidic and an inimitable sweet and sour flavour. An official appellation, protected by a consortium of producers in Modena, reads *Aceto Balsamico Tradizionale di Modena*. Some serious producers bottle a fine product under their own label. The genuine condiment, whether bottled by the consortium or independently by the producer, is very expensive but just a few drops can transform a dish.

There is also the fine quality vinegar to which genuine balsamic has been added. This is less dense, less intense in flavour and less expensive, but it can be excellent for certain dishes. Avoid so-called balsamic vinegars which have been flavoured with sugar or caramel. Again, when in doubt, consult a trusted and knowledgeable fine food grocer.

SOTTACETI AND SOTTOLI

A jar or two of a single vegetable or mixture preserved in fine white wine vinegar, or in olive oil, can be used as part of an antipasto or to garnish cold meat dishes. Several good commercial brands are available in Italian markets. Since the quality of these foods depends on the quality of the vegetables, vinegar and olive oil used, it is safer and more satisfying to make your own.

SPREADS

On Italian labels these pastes are called *paste*. It is especially useful to have on hand good quality pastes made from white and black truffles, *porcini* mushrooms and anchovies.

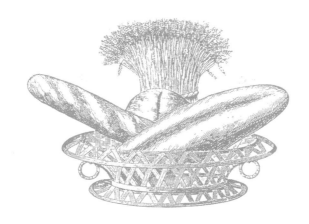

PART II

FINGER FOOD

One advantage to many antipasti is that they can be eaten, if need be, without the support of a plate or the aid of knife, fork and spoon. Some do not even require a napkin, although your guests will probably find one handy.

Finger food is suitable for serving in various situations. It is ideal for cocktail parties, since most of the recipes are quite light. Some are for more substantial dishes, which you might choose if you suspect some of your guests plan to make a meal of the occasion, as we often do at cocktail parties in Italy.

The dishes that are easiest to prepare ahead of time I often serve with an aperitivo *glass of white wine, while we are waiting for all the guests to arrive and I am putting the final touches on my first course before sitting down at table.*

As most finger foods can be served at room temperature they are also appropriate on a buffet table. Of course, any one or combination of these, apart from the little sandwiches, can be enjoyed as an antipasto while seated at the table, especially those that should be eaten warm. You will also find many dishes that make perfect single courses for light luncheons and suppers.

BRUSCHETTE, CROSTINI, TARTINE

THIS FIRST GROUPING OF FINGER FOOD
ANTIPASTI USE BREAD AS THEIR
BASE IN THREE DIFFERENT WAYS.

Bruschette (the "ch" in the middle, I remind my English-speaking students, is pronounced with a hard "k" sound) are grilled slices of bread with a savory topping. By nature they are rustic in texture and appeal and are most suited for informal occasions.

Ideally the bread should be grilled over charcoal on an open fire or at least in an oven. Toasting will do, although it does not give the same taste or texture. The bread should be coarse, country style and fairly thickly cut so it can support the topping. Some toppings can be served in a bowl with the grilled bread apart. I sometimes set the bowl in the centre of a basket and arrange the bread around it and let my guests dress their own.

Of course, there are many other possible toppings for *bruschette*. You can create your own using suitable seasonal produce, broad (fava) beans in the spring, tomatoes in summer, mushrooms in autumn and white beans in the winter. The essential, invariable factor, and I cannot emphasize this enough, is that the olive oil be the best, cold-pressed, extra virgin available. *Crostini* are little toasts with various spreads. They are easy to prepare and versatile to serve, suitable for casual as well as more formal occasions. The bread should be cut from a small, round loaf, what is called a *frusta*, or rod, in Italy. Be sure the type of bread you use does not have holes, since it would not support the spread. It must not be soft but a

little crusty, as the name, *crostini*, implies, and can be toasted or lightly grilled or even a day or so old. Most of these recipes can be served at room temperature but do not prepare them too far in advance as the bread will become soggy.

Crostini are ideal with aperitifs. A platter of three or four mixed *crostini* can also be served at the table as an antipasto. Many can be garnished with a caper or a tiny slice of (bell) pepper. You might also decorate the serving tray with grape or colourful leaves, and arrange the *crostini* on top.

I use the Italian word *tartine* to mean little sandwiches. That is, two slices of bread with a filling in the middle. In some recipe books *tartine* refers to open sandwiches, what the French call *canapes*. It is interesting to note that by the nineteenth century, the English word "sandwich" was used in Italy. The cookery writer Artusi, entitles his antipasto recipe section, *"Crostini e Sandwiches"*.

I use both white and wholewheat bread to make *tartine*. You can cut them into different shapes: square, diagonal and diamond and to make them more delicate, the crust should be cut away. These sandwiches should not be prepared too far ahead of time or they will dry out. It helps to cover them with a slightly damp cloth and keep them in the refrigerator until you are ready to serve.

Pistor. Der Becker.

Importuna fames hominem quemcunq, fatigat;
  Hic Pistoris opem supplice voce petat.
Ille dabit panem tua quo ieiunia pellas,
  Cordis et impasti vim reparare queas.

Viscera continuis ubi fracta laboribus arent,
  Optimus hæc panis fortificare solet.
Omne genus comedas auium, genus omne ferarum,
  Inuenias sapiat quod sine pane nihil.
Artifices igitur multos post terga relinquit,
  Istius et cunctos artis egere patet.

BRUSCHETTA CON BOTTARGA

Bruschetta with Fish Roe

Bottarga is salted pressed fish roe, usually from tuna, but it can also be black lumpfish or red roe. I enjoy eating it with pasta, or mixed with chick-peas or white beans. However you prepare the *bottarga*, make sure it is thinly sliced.

6 large slices coarse country bread, about 1 cm/¹/₂ in thick
150 g/5 oz bottarga
Juice of 1 lemon
3 tbsp extra virgin olive oil
Pepper

Preheat the oven to 180°C/350°F/Gas 4. Place the bread slices on a baking sheet and toast in the oven for about 5 minutes, or until barely golden, turning them just once.
Meanwhile, slice the *bottarga* paper thin then toss with the lemon juice, 2 tbsp of the oil and pepper to taste.
Arrange the toast on individual dishes and brush with the rest of the oil. Cover with the *bottarga* mixture and serve.
Makes 6.

BRUSCHETTA CON MELANZANE E POMODORI

Bruschetta with Aubergine (Eggplant) and Tomatoes

Delicious in summertime when the tomatoes are very ripe, this dish can also be served as a first course or for brunch. There is no need to salt and drain the aubergines (eggplant) as they will lose all their nice taste. Just make sure the ones you use are very fresh.

6 ripe plum tomatoes
1 handful basil leaves
6 tbsp extra virgin olive oil
2 garlic cloves, chopped
2 Japanese-style aubergines (eggplants), long and oval
6 slices coarse country bread, about 1 cm/¹/₂ in thick
Salt and pepper

Peel and chop the tomatoes. Place them in a colander, sprinkle with salt and leave to drain for about 1 hour. Chop the basil and add to the tomatoes, along with 2 tbsp of the oil, the garlic and pepper to taste. Slice the aubergines lengthways, discarding the ends. Brush the slices with 2 tbsp of the oil. Preheat the grill (broiler). Place the aubergines on the grill rack for about 3 minutes each side, or until soft. Add a little salt. Meanwhile, preheat the oven to 180°C/350°F/Gas 4.
Place the bread on a baking sheet and toast in the oven for about 5 minutes, or until barely golden, turning them once. Brush with the rest of the oil, top with the aubergine slices and spoon over the tomatoes. Reheat in the oven for a few minutes, then serve.
Makes 6.

BRUSCHETTA DI RICOTTA

Bruschetta with Ricotta Cheese

This is a very filling antipasto that can be served also as a first course or even a main dish, especially for brunch. I often serve this accompanied by sautéed spinach as a main dish for dinner.

6 slices coarse country bread, about 1 cm/$\frac{1}{2}$ inch thick
2 tbsp extra virgin olive oil
300 g/10 oz/1$\frac{1}{4}$ cups ricotta cheese
2 eggs
120 g/4 oz/1 cup fontina cheese, freshly grated
Pinch grated nutmeg
Salt and pepper

Preheat the oven to 200°C/400°F/Gas 6. Place the bread slices on a baking sheet and toast in the oven for about 2 minutes, or until just warmed through, turning them once. Brush with the oil on one side of each slice.
Meanwhile, mix the ricotta with the eggs, fontina cheese, nutmeg and a little salt and pepper. Stir until smooth and creamy. Place the mixture in a pastry bag with a fluted tip and squeeze on to the toast slices. Return the toast to the oven for about 15 minutes until golden. Serve immediately while still very hot.
Makes 6.

BRUSCHETTA CON FAGIOLI

Bruschetta with White Beans

There are many varieties of white beans called *cannellini* or Great Northerns, but the very best quality in Italy are called *zolfini*. The beans should be simmered very slowly as they are done in Tuscany where most housewives keep wood-burning stoves in the kitchen. They place the pan of beans on the top of the stove, cover and leave over a low heat for a few hours, not even allowing the water to simmer.

210 g/7 oz dried cannellini beans
Few fresh sage leaves
4 tbsp extra virgin olive oil
6 large slices coarse country bread, about 1 cm/$\frac{1}{2}$ in thick
2 garlic cloves
Salt and pepper

Soak the beans in a bowl with enough water to cover for about 12 hours.
When ready to cook, preheat the oven to 200°C/400°F/Gas 6. Drain the beans and place them in a flameproof casserole dish with the sage, 1 tbsp of the oil and enough water to cover about 1 cm/$\frac{1}{2}$ in. Cover and bring to a slow boil on the top of the hob (stove). Place in the oven and simmer for about 3 hours; the beans should be slightly soupy when they are done.
Place the bread slices on a baking sheet and toast in the oven for about 5 minutes, or until barely golden, turning them over once. Rub with the garlic and arrange on individual dishes. Spoon the beans on top and sprinkle with salt and pepper to taste and the rest of the oil. Serve immediately while still hot.
Makes 6.

BRUSCHETTA ALLA SALSICCIA

Bruschetta with Sausages

The sausage *ragú* in this recipe is excellent on a *bruschetta*, but can also double as a perfect, tasty *spaghetti* or *fettuccine* sauce.

300 g/10 oz sweet Italian sausages
210 g/7 oz lean boneless pork meat
1 small carrot
1 celery stalk
1 small onion
4 ripe plum tomatoes
4 tbsp extra virgin olive oil
1 tbsp fennel seeds
6 tbsp dry white wine
1 tbsp fresh thyme leaves
6 large slices coarse country bread, 1 cm/^{1}/$_2$ in thick
Salt and pepper

Peel the sausages and crumble the meat into a bowl. Finely chop the pork, carrot, celery and onion. Peel and chop the tomatoes.

Heat the oil in a frying pan. Add the carrot, celery and onion and cook over a medium heat for about 3 minutes, stirring constantly, or until the onion is translucent. Stir in the sausage meat and pork and continue cooking for a further 3 minutes. Add the fennel seeds, tomatoes, wine, thyme, salt and pepper to taste. Cover the pan, lower the heat to a minimum and cook for about 1 hour, stirring from time to time and adding a little water if necessary to keep moist.

Uncover and let the juices evaporate completely. Meanwhile, preheat the oven to 180°C/350°F/Gas 4. Place the bread slices on a baking sheet and toast in the oven for about 5 minutes, or until barely golden, turning them once. Brush with the rest of the oil and arrange on individual dishes. Spread with the sausage *ragú* and serve immediately while still very hot.
Makes 6.

BRUSCHETTA AI PEPERONI

Bruschetta with (Bell) Peppers

The (bell) peppers have a peel that is unpleasant only when they are sautéed. I like to leave the peel on when the peppers are cooked in the oven, as in this recipe. It does not disturb me, but if you want to peel them after they come out of the oven, place them in a closed paper bag for about 10 minutes to loosen the peels so they are easier to peel off.

3 yellow (bell) peppers
3 tbsp extra virgin olive oil
3 garlic cloves, chopped
1 handful fresh basil leaves, shredded
6 large slices coarse country bread, about 1 cm/^{1}/$_2$ inch thick
Salt and pepper

Preheat the oven to 180°C/350°F/Gas 4. Cut the peppers in half, discard the seeds and cores and arrange, cut side up, on a baking sheet brushed with 1 tbsp of the oil. Roast in the oven for about 40 minutes. Sprinkle with salt and pepper and let them cool slightly.

Pour over 1 tbsp of the oil, the garlic and the basil. Meanwhile, brush the bread slices on both sides with the rest of the oil and toast them in the oven for about 5 minutes, or until barely golden, turning them once. Arrange the toast slices on individual dishes, top with the peppers and serve.
Makes 6.

Opposite page: Bruschetta with (Bell) Peppers

BRUSCHETTA DI CAVOLFIORE

Bruschetta with Cauliflower

Cabbage varieties such as cauliflower, broccoli and savoy cabbage originated in Europe and were very popular in ancient Rome, being one of the few winter vegetables available at that time. You can substitute broccoli for the cauliflower.

600 g/1¼ lb cauliflower
6 tbsp extra virgin olive oil
6 large slices coarse country bread, 1 cm/½ in thick
2 garlic cloves
Salt and pepper

Bring a large pan of salted water to the boil. Add the cauliflower and cook for about 10 minutes. Drain well and when cool enough to handle divide the cauliflower into florets.
Heat 3 tbsp of the oil in a large frying pan. Add the cauliflower and sauté for about 5 minutes over medium heat, stirring the florets delicately a couple of times. Add salt and pepper to taste.
Meanwhile, preheat the oven to 180°C/350°F/Gas 4. Place the bread slices on a baking sheet and toast in the oven for about 5 minutes, or until barely golden, turning them once. Rub with the garlic, then arrange on individual dishes. Pour over the rest of the oil. Cover with the cauliflower and serve very hot.
Makes 6.

BRUSCHETTA AL TARTUFO

Bruschetta with White Truffle

Called the "diamond of the kitchen" during the Renaissance, white truffle remains one of our most precious ingredients. Traditionally harvested from November through January, truffles always command a premium price because only specially trained dogs can sniff them out. Now a species called *Scorzone* are sold all year round. Although they look like truffles, I don't think they have anything of the very strong and characteristic perfume.

1 white truffle, about 120 g/4 oz
6 large slices coarse country bread, about 1 cm/½ in thick
45 g/1½ oz/3 tbsp unsalted butter, at room temperature
90 g/3 oz/6 tbsp freshly grated Parmesan cheese

Preheat the oven to 200°C/400°F/Gas 6. Brush off the dirt from the truffle; *never* wash a truffle. Arrange the bread slices in a buttered ovenproof dish and spread one side of each with 30 g/1 oz/2 tbsp of the butter. Shave the truffle over the bread. Cover with the cheese and dot with the rest of the butter. Roast for about 10 minutes or until the toast is golden and the cheese has melted and is bubbling. Serve immediately, while still very hot.
Makes 6.

BRUSCHETTA AI CARCIOFI

Bruschetta with Artichokes

The best artichokes I can buy in Tuscany are called *morellini*, very small with no choke and leaves so tender that it is a waste to discard them. Another good quality variety is the *mammoli*, a little bigger but without any thorns.

As the artichokes aren't cooked in this recipe it is essential to use only the very young, tender varieties.

6 large slices coarse country bread, about 1 cm/^{1}/$_2$ in thick
6 artichokes
Juice of 1 lemon
120 g/4 oz parmesan cheese, in one piece
3 tbsp extra virgin olive oil
Salt and pepper

Preheat the oven to 180°C/350°F /Gas 4. Place the bread slices on a baking sheet and toast them in the oven for about 5 minutes, or until barely golden, turning them just once.
Meanwhile, clean the artichokes, discarding the tough leaves and furry choke. Slice them thinly lengthways, dropping the slices into a bowl of water with the lemon juice to prevent discolouration. Shave the parmesan.
Drain the artichoke slices and pat dry in a towel. Arrange the toast on individual dishes and cover with the artichokes slices and the shaved parmesan cheese. Sprinkle with salt and pepper, pour over the olive oil and serve.
Makes 6.

BRUSCHETTA ALLA CAVOLELLA E ACCIUGHE

Bruschetta with Sautéed Cabbage and Anchovies

During cold weather, this is a very popular antipasto here at the Badia a Coltibuono restaurant. Use a round and firm white head of cabbage. This variety of cabbage – used to make coleslaw – is very popular in Italy, always served thinly sliced with oil, vinegar and salt as one would eat raw lettuce.

6 large slices coarse country bread, about 1 cm/^{1}/$_2$ in thick
300 g/10 oz cabbage
6 tbsp extra virgin olive oil
3 garlic cloves, chopped
3 anchovy fillets in oil, drained
2 tbsp red wine vinegar
Salt and pepper

Preheat a grill (broiler). Toast the bread, turning the slices just once until barely golden. Meanwhile, slice the cabbage very thinly.
Heat 3 tbsp of the oil in a large frying pan over a medium heat. Add the garlic and anchovies and sauté for 2 minutes. Add the cabbage, the vinegar, salt and pepper to taste. Mix quickly to just barely wilt the cabbage.
Arrange the toasted bread slices on individual dishes and cover with the cabbage. Pour over the rest of the oil and serve immediately while still very hot.
Makes 6.

CROSTINI DI SPADA

Swordfish Crostini

This is a very delicate fish *carpaccio*, seasoned with balsamic vinegar, on top of the *crostini*. The fish should be sliced paper thin, and tuna or salmon can be substituted for the swordfish. Place the fish in the freezer for about 30 minutes to make slicing easy.

12 slices Italian country-style bread, such as frusta, about 0.5 cm/¼ in thick
3 tbsp extra virgin olive oil
3 tbsp balsamic vinegar
120 g/4 oz swordfish fillets, sliced paper thin
12 paper-thin slices lemon, with peel
1 tbsp finely chopped fresh flat-leaf parsley
Salt and pepper

Preheat the oven to 180°C/350°F/Gas 4. Place the sliced bread on a baking sheet and toast in the oven for about 5 minutes or until barely golden, turning them once. Allow to cool to room temperature. Brush the toast with 1 tbsp of the oil.
Make a marinade with the balsamic vinegar, the rest of the oil and a little salt and pepper to taste. Dip the swordfish in the marinade to coat well. Top each piece of toast with a slice of lemon and cover with some fish. Sprinkle with the parsley and serve.
Makes 12.

CROSTINI AI FUNGHI

Toasts with Porcini Mushrooms

Porcini mushrooms are not easily found in the wild, often only a few people will know where they are and they prefer to keep this a secret. *Porcini* grow abundantly around Coltibuono when they are in season and I like to go and pick them with my grandchildren.

These *crostini* are delicious warm. Have all the ingredients ready so you can top with the mushrooms and reheat in the oven just before serving.

12 slices Italian country-style bread, such as frusta, about 0.5 cm/¼ in thick
300 g/10 oz fresh porcini, shittake or button mushrooms
3 tbsp extra virgin olive oil
3 garlic cloves left whole
12 thin slices fontina cheese
Salt and pepper

Preheat the oven to 180°C/350°F/Gas 4. Place the slices of bread on 1 or 2 baking sheets and toast in the oven for about 3 minutes, or until barely golden, turning them once. Leave to cool to room temperature.
Clean the mushrooms and slice thinly.
Heat the oil with the garlic in a frying pan. Add the mushrooms and sauté over a high heat for about 5 minutes, stirring a couple of times. Add salt and pepper to taste and remove the pan from the heat. Cut the fontina with a pastry (biscuit) cutter the size of the toast. Arrange the fontina on top of the toast. Just before serving, add the mushrooms and return to the oven for about 3 minutes or until the cheese starts to melt. Arrange on a platter and serve immediately, while still hot.
Makes 12.

CROSTINI AL TONNO

Toasts with Tuna

Because these tasty *crostini* are so simple and fast to make, they are one of my favourites. Canned tuna is very popular in Italy, and we use it for making sauces, pasta and filling vegetables.

Tuna is also the main ingredient in a dish called *Finto Pesce*. This is a fake fish made from mashed potato, mayonnaise and canned tuna, moulded into the shape of a fish with capers for eyes. This was a treat in my mother's house when I was a little girl.

12 slices Italian country-style bread, such as frusta, about 0.5 cm/¹/₄ in thick
240 g/8 oz canned tuna in oil
Yolks of 3 hard-cooked eggs
45 g/1¹/₂ oz/3 tbsp unsalted butter, softened
2 tbsp lemon juice
2 anchovy fillets in oil
12 paper-thin slices lemon with peel on
12 capers in salt, rinsed

Preheat the oven to 180°C/350°F/Gas 4. Place the slices of bread on 1 or 2 baking sheets and toast in the oven for about 3 minutes or until barely golden, turning them once; allow to cool to room temperature.
Put the tuna with its oil, the egg yolks, butter, lemon juice and anchovy fillets in a food processor and process until a smooth paste forms. Spread the paste on the toast and top with the lemon slices. Arrange a caper in the centre of each. Arrange on a platter and serve.
Makes 12.

CROSTINI DI CREMA
DI SARDINE

Crostini with Cream of Sardines

You can use a commercial mayonnaise to prepare these *crostini*, but I usually like to make it myself. It only takes a minute in the food processor and keeps for a few days in the refrigerator.

12 slices Italian country-style bread, such as frusta, about 0.5 cm/¹/₄ in thick
5 canned sardines
6 tbsp Mayonnaise (page 177), or good-quality commercial
2 anchovy fillets in oil, drained
3 drops Worcestershire sauce
1 tbsp capers in vinegar, drained

Preheat the oven to 180°C/350°F/Gas 4. Place the slices of bread on 1 or 2 baking sheets and toast in the oven for about 3 minutes, or until barely golden, turning them once. Leave the toast to cool to room temperature.
Place the sardines, mayonnaise, anchovy fillets, Worcestershire sauce and capers in a food processor and process until a smooth paste forms.
Spread the sardine cream on the toast. Arrange on a platter and serve.
Makes 12.

CROSTINI AL CARPACCIO E RUCOLA

Beef Carpaccio and Rocket (Arugula) Toasts

Topside or eye round of beef are ideal cuts for this recipe. Keep the meat in the freezer for about 30 minutes to be able to slice it paper thin. The rocket (arugula) should be shredded very finely by hand, never chopped in a machine.

12 slices Italian country-style bread, such as frusta, 0.5 cm/¹/₄ in thick
12 slices lean topside or eye round beef, sliced paper thin
Juice of 2 lemons
3 tbsp extra virgin olive oil
3 drops hot pepper sauce
90 g/3 oz rocket (arugula) finely shredded
Salt and pepper

Preheat the oven to 180°C/350°F/Gas 4. Place the bread slices on a baking sheet and toast in the oven for about 3 minutes, or until barely golden, turning them once; let cool to room temperature.
Put the lemon juice in a glass bowl, add the meat and leave for about 30 minutes, turning the meat a couple of times. Brush the toasts with 1 tbsp of the oil.
Meanwhile, mix the rest of the oil in a dish with the hot pepper sauce and a little salt and pepper to taste. Drain the meat from the lemon and dip each slice in the oil mixture to coat evenly. Distribute on top of the toast and cover with the rocket (arugula). Arrange on a platter and serve.
Makes 12.

CROSTINI DI RUCOLA AL BALSAMICO

Crostini with Rocket (Arugula) and Balsamic Vinegar

You can substitute another fresh herb, such as tarragon, parsley, basil or chives, for the rocket (arugula).

1 handful rocket (arugula)
12 slices Italian country-style bread, such as frusta, about 0.5 cm/¹/₄ in thick
210 g/7 oz/³/₄ cup plus 2 tbsp ricotta cheese
3 spring onions (scallions), finely chopped
15 g/¹/₂ oz/1 tbsp unsalted butter at room temperature
1 tbsp lemon juice
1 tbsp balsamic vinegar
Salt and pepper

Chop the rocket (arugula) finely, reserving a few leaves for garnishing. Set aside.
Preheat the oven to 180°C/350°F/Gas 4. Place the slices of bread on 1 or 2 baking sheets and toast in the oven for about 3 minutes, or until barely golden, turning them once; allow to cool to room temperature.
Cream the ricotta cheese with a fork, adding the spring onions (scallions), butter, lemon juice, balsamic vinegar, salt and pepper to taste. Stir in the chopped rocket. Spread the toast with the ricotta mixture. Thinly slice the rest of the rocket and garnish each *crostini*. Serve immediately.
Makes 12.

Opposite page: Beef Carpaccio and Rocket (Arugula) Toasts

CROSTINI ALLA MOZZARELLA

Mozzarella Toasts

Authentic buffalo mozzarella comes from Campania and is made only in small quantities in the springtime. It has a unique taste and texture. When it is fresh it will be very white. Due to the recent popularity, however, it is now made commercially with cows' milk and you can buy decent imitations made in Italy or the United States.

12 slices Italian country-style bread such as frusta, about
0.5 cm/^{1}/$_4$ in thick
350 g/12 oz mozzarella cheese, of the best quality
you can find
6 anchovy fillets in oil, drained and rinsed
1 tbsp extra virgin olive oil
1 tsp dried oregano
Pepper

Preheat the oven to 180°C/350°F/Gas 4. Place the slices of bread on 1 or 2 baking sheets and toast in the oven for about 3 minutes, or until barely golden, turning them once.
Cut the mozzarella into 12 slices and slice the anchovy fillets lengthwise.
Brush the toast with the oil and cover each slice with a slice of mozzarella. Roll up the anchovy fillets and arrange in the centre. Sprinkle with the oregano and pepper. Serve immediately; do not let stand too long because the bread will become soggy.
Makes 12.

CROSTINI DI GAMBERETTI

Crostini with Prawns (Shrimp)

The mayonnaise in this recipe becomes bright green with fennel and parsley, and topped with the prawns (shrimp) makes a very elegant antipasto. Everything can be prepared ahead of time and assembled at the last minute.

12 prawns (shrimp), peeled and deveined
12 slices Italian country-style bread, such as frusta, about
0.5 cm/^{1}/$_4$ in thick
12 tbsp Mayonnaise (page 177), or good quality commercial
2 hard-cooked eggs, shelled and chopped
1 tbsp finely chopped fresh fennel fronds
2 tbsp finely chopped fresh flat-leaf parsley

Cook the prawns (shrimp) in boiling water for 2 minutes. Drain well and leave to cool.
Preheat the oven to 180°C/350°F/Gas 4. Place the slices of bread on 1 or 2 baking sheets and toast in the oven for about 3 minutes, or until barely golden, turning them once; allow to cool to room temperature.
Meanwhile, mix the mayonnaise with the eggs, fennel and parsley. Spread generously on the toast. Arrange the prawns on the toast and serve.
Makes 12.

CROSTINI DI POLENTA AL FORMAGGIO

Polenta Crostini with Goats' Cheese and Chives

This is a very nice antipasto that can be served with a glass of white wine while your guests are still in the sitting room waiting for the meal. You can also replace the goats' cheese with a slice of fontina cheese sprinkled with sweet paprika. The polenta for this recipe cooks in only 10 minutes because it is made with less water than usual and it cooks again in the oven.

300g/10 oz/2 cups polenta (yellow cornmeal)
1.3 ltr/2^1/$_2$ pints/6 cups water
3 tbsp extra virgin olive oil
180g/6 oz fresh goats' cheese
2 tbsp chopped fresh chives
Salt

Prepare polenta following the recipe for basic polenta (page 180), using the cornmeal and 1.3 ltr/2^1/$_2$ pts/6 cups water. Spoon it on a wet work surface and press down with your wet hands. Flatten with a wet rolling pin until about 0.5 cm/^{1}/$_4$ in thick, then leave to cool completely.
Meanwhile, preheat the oven to 180°C/350°F/Gas 4. Cut the polenta into 5 cm/2 in rounds using a pastry (biscuit) cutter dipped in water to prevent sticking. Brush a baking sheet with a little of the oil, then arrange the polenta rounds, in a single layer, on top. Brush the tops with half of the remaining oil. Toast in the oven for about 10 minutes. Turn the polenta rounds over and brush with the rest of the oil. Toast for a further 5 minutes until barely golden.
Meanwhile, put the cheese in a pastry bag with a large fluted tip. Squeeze dots of the cheese on top of the polenta toasts. Return them to the oven for a couple of minutes longer. Sprinkle with the chives. Arrange on a platter and serve immediately, while still very hot.
Makes 30.

CROSTINI AI CAPRINI E CETRIOLI

Crostini with Goats' Cheese and Cucumbers

Cucumber was a very popular ingredient in ancient Egypt. The Pharaohs fed them to the people building the pyramids, probably because of the high water content, which makes them ideal in a warm and dry climate.

1 cucumber, peeled and diced
12 slices Italian country-style bread, such as frusta, about 0.5 cm/^{1}/$_4$ in thick
300 g/10 oz fresh goats' cheese
2 tbsp finely snipped fresh chives
3 tbsp extra virgin olive oil
Salt and pepper

Salt the cucumber in a colander and allow to rest for about 1 hour. Remove and pat dry.
Meanwhile, preheat the oven to 180°C/350°F/Gas 4. Place the slices of bread on 1 or 2 baking sheets and toast in the oven for about 3 minutes, or until barely golden, turning them once. Leave to cool to room temperature.
Mix together the goats' cheese, chives, oil and pepper to taste. Put the cream in a pastry bag with a large fluted tip. Layer the cucumber on top of the toast, then pipe on the cheese. Serve immediately.
Makes 12.

CROSTINI DI POLENTA E BACCALÀ

Polenta and Baccalà Crostini

These *crostini* can also be served as a first course, if you arrange them slightly overlapping on an ovenproof serving dish and heat in a 180°C/350°F/Gas 4 oven for about 20 minutes before serving. *Baccalà* is salted cod, which you will find in Italian delicatessens and some fish markets. If you can't find any, top the *crostini* with slices of fontina cheese and maybe a little sliced white truffle.

300 g/10 oz baccalà
300 g/10 oz/2 cups coarse polenta (yellow cornmeal)
1.3 ltr/2^1/$_2$ pints/6 cups water
120 ml/4 fl oz/^{1}/$_2$ cup extra virgin olive oil
1 tbsp finely chopped fresh flat-leaf parsley
Salt

Keep the *baccalà* covered with abundant water for 24 hours, changing the water at least 6 times. Drain and carefully remove the bones. Set aside. To make polenta, bring the water to the boil. Add salt and the polenta in a steady stream, stirring constantly with a wooden spoon. Continue to cook, covered, over a low heat for about 10 minutes. Wet a work surface with water and pour the polenta on top. Flatten with a wet rolling pin until about 0.5 cm/^{1}/$_4$ in thick, then leave to cool completely. Cut into 5 cm/2 in rounds using a pastry (biscuit) cutter dipped in water to prevent sticking.
Preheat the oven to 180°C/350°F/Gas 4. Brush both sides of the polenta rounds with 2 tbsp of the oil. Arrange on a baking sheet and toast in the oven for about 20 minutes, turning them once, until crusty and barely golden.
Meanwhile, cream the *baccalà* with the rest of the oil, beating it in with a wooden spoon in a thin stream. This is the same technique as for making mayonnaise by hand (page 177). Stir in the parsley. Spoon on top of the polenta slices and serve immediately.
Makes 18.

CROSTINI CON AVOCADO E GORGONZOLA

Crostini with Avocado and Gorgonzola

This unusual topping is quite tasty. For an attractive garnish, I arrange these *crostini* on a bed of lettuce leaves. When gorgonzola is fresh, it is very white and not too smelly.

12 slices Italian country-style bread, such as frusta, about 0.5 cm/^{1}/$_4$ in thick
2 avocados
120 g/7 oz very fresh gorgonzola cheese
1 tsp grated lemon zest

Preheat the oven to 180°C/350°F/Gas 4. Place the slices of bread on 1 or 2 baking sheets and toast in the oven for about 3 minutes, or until barely golden, turning them once.
Halve the avocados, discard the stones (pits), then peel them. Mash the flesh with a fork until smooth and creamy. Stir in the gorgonzola cheese and lemon zest until well combined. Spread on the toast and serve immediately.
Makes 12.

TARTINE AL TONNO E CETRIOLINI

Tuna and Cucumber Sandwiches

The very small cucumbers preserved in vinegar used in this recipe are readily available in Italian delicatessens.

210 g/7 oz canned tuna in oil or brine, drained
30 g/1 oz small cucumbers in vinegar, drained
1 tbsp capers in vinegar, drained
1 egg yolk
1 canned anchovy fillet, drained
3 tbsp extra virgin olive oil
6 lettuce leaves
12 slices Pane Bianco (page 185), or shop-bought white bread

Put the tuna, cucumbers, capers, egg yolk, anchovy fillet and olive oil in a food processor and process until smooth and creamy. Set aside. Trim the lettuce leaves to the size of the bread slices.
Spread the tuna mixture on top of 6 slices of bread and then top with the lettuce. Top with the rest of the bread and press lightly together. Cut each sandwich in half. Arrange on a platter and serve.
Makes 12 halves.

TARTINE AL PROSCIUTTO COTTO

Ham Sandwiches

I usually make this sandwich spread with butter, but the butter can be easily replaced with ricotta for a lighter creation. If you do this, it is important to cream the ricotta in a blender before mixing it with the fontina and ham.

180 g/6 oz cooked ham
2 anchovy fillets in brine or oil, drained
60 g/2 oz unsalted butter, softened
60 g/2 oz/^{1}/$_2$ cup fontina cheese, freshly grated
12 slices Pane Bianco (page 185), or shop-bought white bread

Place the ham and anchovies in a food processor and process. Cream the butter with a fork until soft and smooth. Stir in the cheese and the ham mixture until well blended.
Spread the mixture on top of half the slices of bread. Top with the rest of the slices and press lightly together. Cut each sandwich in half diagonally.
Arrange on a platter and serve.
Makes 12 halves.

TARTINE AI GAMBERETTI

Prawn (Shrimp) Sandwiches

You can easily substitute sautéed scallops, boiled lobster or crabmeat, or any leftover cooked fish, for the prawns (shrimp).

180 g/6 oz peeled and deveined prawns (shrimp)
90 g/3 oz/6 tbsp mascarpone cheese
1 large egg yolk
Juice of ^{1}/$_2$ lemon
1 tbsp finely chopped fresh flat-leaf parsley
12 slices Pane Bianco (page 185), or shop-bought white bread
Salt and pepper

Bring a large pan of water to the boil. Add the prawns (shrimp) and the salt and cook for just 2 minutes; drain. Put the prawns in a blender with the mascarpone cheese, egg yolk, lemon juice, parsley and pepper to taste and process until creamy.
Spread half the bread slices with the prawn mixture. Top with the rest of the bread and press together lightly with your hands. Cut each sandwich in half. Arrange on a platter and serve.
Makes 12 halves.

TARTINE AL POLLO

Brown Bread Chicken Sandwiches

A classic Italian recipe for cooking chicken breasts is used to fill these sandwiches. To make them even tastier I add some very finely julienned lettuce leaves and finely chopped fresh parsley.

45 g/1¹/₂ oz/3 tbsp unsalted butter, softened
1 tbsp extra virgin olive oil
2 skinless chicken breasts (halves), thinly sliced
4 tbsp marsala wine
2 tbsp sweet mustard
12 slices Pane Nero (page 184), or shop-bought wholemeal (wholewheat) bread
3 lettuce leaves, finely julienned
1 tbsp finely chopped fresh flat-leaf parsley
Salt and pepper

Melt 15 g/¹/₂ oz/1 tbsp of the butter with the oil in a frying pan (skillet). Add the chicken breasts and sauté for a few minutes over a high heat until golden, stirring and turning over occasionally with a wooden spoon. Add the marsala and salt and pepper to taste and cook over a low heat for about 5 minutes, or until the liquid evaporates and the chicken breasts are tender and cooked through. Remove from the pan and allow to cool.
Meanwhile, cream the rest of the butter with the mustard and spread over half the bread slices. Cover with the julienned lettuce and the chicken slices. Sprinkle with the parsley and top with the rest of the bread. Press together lightly with the palm of your hand. Cut each sandwich in half. Arrange on a platter and serve.
Makes 12 halves.

TARTINE AL FINOCCHIO

Fennel Sandwiches

The fontina cheese used for these sandwiches can be replaced with emmenthal or gruyère. I sometimes also mix the cooked fennel with ricotta cheese.

2 tbsp extra virgin olive oil
1 small onion, thinly sliced
2 fennel bulbs, thinly sliced
¹/₂ tsp powdered saffron (optional)
6 slices of fontina cheese, same size as bread
12 slices Pane Nero (page 184) or shop-bought wholemeal (whole-wheat) bread
Salt and pepper

Heat the oil in a saucepan. Add the onion and fennel and cook over a low heat for about 5 minutes, stirring occasionally. Add salt and pepper to taste and a little water. Cover and continue cooking for a further 10 minutes, or until the fennel is very soft. Stir in the saffron and continue cooking until all the liquid evaporates. Allow to cool to room temperature.
Arrange the fontina cheese and fennel on half the slices of thebread, then top with the rest of the bread. Press lightly together with the palm of your hand. Cut each sandwich in half. Arrange on a platter and serve.
Makes 12 halves.

TARTINE DI CARNE

Meat Terrine Sandwiches

These sandwiches are my grandson's favourite. He is a real meat lover and likes to eat these after we go mushroom picking in the woods.

90 g/3 oz lean boneless veal
90 g/3 oz chicken breast fillet
90 g/3 oz cooked ham
3 large egg yolks (U.S. extra large)
45 g/1½ oz/3 tbsp Parmesan cheese, freshly grated
45 g/1½ oz/3 tbsp unsalted butter
1 handful pistachio nuts, shelled
12 slices Pane Bianco (page 185) or Pane Nero (page 184) or shop-bought white or wholemeal (wholewheat) bread
Salt and pepper

Preheat the oven to 190°C/375°F/Gas 5.
Put the veal, chicken and ham in a food processor fitted with a metal blade and process until finely chopped. Add the egg yolks, the Parmesan, 30 g/1 oz/2 tbsp of the butter and salt and pepper to taste and process until creamy. Stir in the pistachios.
With the rest of the butter, generously coat a rectangular mould about 23 cm/9 in long, then fill with the mixture. Place the mould in a roasting pan filled with 2.5 cm/1 in hot water. Cover and cook in the oven for about 45 minutes. Remove from the oven and uncover. Weight down the terrine and allow to cool completely, this will take a couple of hours. Unmould and slice. Arrange the slices on top of half the bread, cover with the rest of the bread and press lightly together. Cut each sandwich in half. Arrange on a platter and serve.
Makes 12 halves.

TARTINE DI FUNGHI E SPINACI

Wild Porcini Mushroom and Spinach Sandwiches

The wild *porcini* season is not very long, lasting only from July to November, and the harvest is best in warm weather after a good rain. If you pick the mushrooms in the woods never use plastic bags to hold them. Instead, carry your pickings in straw baskets, which allow the spores to feed the ground again. You can also use fresh button mushrooms in this, but the flavour will be less intense.

120 g/4 oz porcini or button mushrooms
120 g/4 oz very fresh, small spinach leaves
3 tbsp extra virgin olive oil
1 tbsp lemon juice
30 g/1 oz parmesan cheese, thinly sliced
12 slices Pane Bianco (page 185) or Pane Nero (page 184), or shop-bought white or wholemeal (wholewheat) bread
Salt and pepper

Slice the mushrooms very thinly. Mix the mushrooms and spinach with the oil, lemon juice, parmesan and salt and pepper to taste.
Cover half the bread slices with the mushroom mixture. Top with the rest of the slices and press together lightly with your hands. Cut each sandwich in half diagonally. Arrange on a platter and serve.
Makes 12 halves.

TARTINE DI FRITTATA

Omelet Sandwiches

For variety the frittata can also be seasoned with fried sage, fresh rosemary, thyme, tarragon, parsley or coriander (cilantro).

3 tbsp extra virgin olive oil
2 small courgettes (zucchini), finely chopped
1 handful fresh basil leaves, chopped
60 g/2 oz/4 tbsp freshly grated parmesan cheese
3 large eggs (U.S. extra large)
12 slices or Pane Nero (page 184), or shop-bought wholemeal (wholewheat) bread
Salt and pepper

Heat 2 tbsp of the oil in a frying pan. Add the courgettes (zucchini) and sauté over a medium heat for about 5 minutes, until the courgettes are wilted and tender, stirring occasionally. Stir in the basil, cheese, salt and pepper to taste; leave to cool to room temperature.

Beat the eggs, then mix with the courgettes. Heat the rest of the oil in a large frying pan. Pour in the egg mixture and cook on one side over medium heat until the eggs are almost set. Flip the frittata over and cook on the other side for just 1 minute. Slide the frittata out of the pan and leave to cool.

Cut the frittata into 6 large pieces, then use to top half of the bread slices. Cover with the rest of the bread. Cut each sandwich in half diagonally. Arrange on a platter and serve.
Makes 12 halves.

TARTINE AL CAVIALE ROSSO

Red Caviar Sandwich

I worked out this simple recipe years ago in Iran when I was invited by the Shah's wife to a children's film festival. It was too expensive to buy beluga so I substituted red fish roe. Red caviar or any good fish roe – and if you really want to be extravagant beluga caviar – are wonderful ingredients for the sandwich, and the ricotta cheese adds substance.

180 g/6 oz red caviar or other fish roe
180 g/6 oz/3/4 cup ricotta cheese
Juice of 1 lemon
12 slices Pane Bianco (page 185), or shop-bought white bread

Very delicately, in order not to break the eggs, stir together the roe, ricotta and lemon juice until well blended. Spread over half the bread slices and top with the rest of the bread. Press together lightly with the palm of your hand. Cut each sandwich in half. Arrange on a platter and serve.
Makes 12 halves.

TARTINE AL GORGONZOLA

Gorgonzola Sandwiches

You can use roquefort or other blue cheese instead of gorgonzola, but in that case beat the cheese with some ricotta or mascarpone cheese to make it creamier.

180 g/6 oz gorgonzola cheese
60 g/2 oz/1/2 cup shelled walnuts, chopped
Juice of 1/2 lemon
12 slices Pane Bianco (page 185) or Pane Nero (page 184), or shop-bought white or wholemeal (wholewheat) bread

Cream the gorgonzola well with the walnuts and the lemon juice. Spread the mixture on half the bread slices and top with the rest of the slices. Press together lightly with the palm of your hand. Cut each sandwich in half and arrange on a platter.
Makes 12 halves.

Opposite page: Omelette Sandwiches

Bocconcini, Crocchette, Ripieni

These three types of finger food take a little more preparation and are more filling. Since they do not have bread as a support, some of these dishes will require toothpicks or skewers as a handle. Others should be shaped into finger-manageable forms, little packets or rolls, etc.

Bocconcini, literally *"little mouthfuls"*, are bite-sized morsels of just about any tasty food that can stand on their own, whether raw, fried, baked or boiled. In northern Italy *bocconcini* is also the name of a veal stew.

Crocchette comes from the French, *croquettes*, and the Italian word means the same thing, something that is crispy, crackling and crunchy. These are mostly fried dishes. Traditionally *béchamel* was used to bind the ingredients but sometimes I prefer a lighter version and use rice or polenta. Fry evenly with a light touch so that they will look attractive on the platter.

Ripieni, filled and stuffed morsels, make up some of the most inventive finger-food antipasti. You can play at combining different flavours and textures. They are also a good way to use leftovers. Vegetables are the principal ingredient in these dishes, stuffed with cheese, fish and meat.

Different and delicious are the recipes for *ravioli* and *gnocchi*, traditional first courses, here prepared and served as antipasti. Since all these dishes are meant to be eaten with the fingers, keep in mind they must be cooked to just the right consistency, not too soft, nor have too much liquid.

Tra le celebrazioni della "polenta" che anche quest'anno si sono svolte in varie parti d'Italia, caratteristica per entusiasmo e giocondità è quella avvenuta a Ponti (Alessandria). Ecco il momento in cui più accanito ferve il lavoro dei molti cuochi improvvisati, che distribuiranno poi la polenta alla popolazione. (Disegno di A. Beltrame)

BOCCONCINI AL SALMONE AFFUMICATO

Smoked Salmon Bites

Horseradish is a popular ingredient in the north east of Italy, especially with boiled meat, smoked ham or sausages. Even though horseradish is readily available prepared in small jars, I usually buy the whole radish. After peeling it, I put it in a blender to chop as finely as possible with a little lemon juice to keep it white. If you want to soften the taste, add a little whipped cream.

8 cauliflower florets
120 g/4 oz fresh goats' cheese
1 tbsp finely chopped fresh horseradish
2 hard-cooked eggs, shelled and chopped
8 smoked salmon slices

Bring a large pan of water to the boil. Add salt and the cauliflower florets and blanch for about 3 minutes; drain and allow to cool.

Meanwhile, cream the goats' cheese with the horseradish and the chopped eggs. Spread the cheese mixture on top of the salmon slices, then top with the florets. Wrap the salmon around the floret and secure with a cocktail stick (toothpick). Arrange on a platter and chill until ready to serve.

Makes 8.

BOCCONCINI DI PROSCIUTTO E FONTINA

Ham and Fontina Cheese Bites

This very nice flavourful combination can be served hot or at room temperature. The pear in the centre can be replaced with a slice of apple or peach in summertime or, naturally, melon.

8 chives
180 g/6 oz fontina or emmenthal cheese
2 Bosch pears
8 slices prosciutto

Bring a pan of water to the boil. Add the chives and blanch for 1 minute to soften. Drain, refresh under cold water and pat dry. Julienne the fontina cheese.

Peel, core and divide the pears into 8 pieces. Arrange a piece of cheese and a piece of pear on each slice of *prosciutto*. Fold over the ham to form little square packages. Tie closed with the chives as if they were ribbons, making little knots. Arrange the packages on a platter and chill until ready to serve.

If you want to serve these hot, heat them in an ovenproof dish in a preheated 190°C/375°F/Gas 5 oven for 10 minutes until the fontina cheese is just melting. Arrange on a platter and serve immediately.

Makes 8.

BOCCONCINI DI SEDANO AL FORMAGGIO

Celery and Cheese Bites

Raw celery is excellent and tender, providing you remove the string along the stalk. You can also use the cream cheese as a dip for the celery, rather than piping it.

6 large white celery stalks
2 hard-cooked eggs, shelled and chopped
1 small onion, finely chopped
180 g/6 oz fresh goats' cheese, or other creamy cheese
1 tbsp snipped fresh chives
Pepper

Peel the celery stalks using a vegetable peeler or sharp knife to remove the strings, then cut them in 18 pieces about 5 cm/2 in long; set aside.

Combine with the onion and cheese and stir until creamy. Add pepper to taste.

Fill a pastry bag fitted with a fluted end with the mixture. Pipe on to the celery pieces to fill the cavities. Sprinkle with the chives. Arrange on a platter and chill until ready to serve.

Makes 18.

BOCCONCINI DI POLLO

Chicken Bites

You can replace the *prosciutto* with sliced *mortadella* or paper-thin slices of fontina cheese. I like to serve these hot, but when there is no time, they are also excellent cold.

2 skinless chicken breasts (halved)
6 tbsp extra virgin olive oil
1 tbsp juniper berries, lightly crushed
2 garlic cloves, finely chopped
1 clove
Few fresh sage leaves
1 sprig rosemary
15 g/^{1}/$_2$ oz/1 tbsp unsalted butter
60 ml/2 fl oz/^{1}/$_4$ cup dry white wine
180 g/6 oz prosciutto
1 handful chive stems, blanched for 1 minute and drained
Salt and pepper

Dice the chicken into 5 cm/2 in pieces. Put them in a bowl with the oil, berries, garlic, clove, sage, rosemary and salt and pepper to taste. Leave to marinate for about 2 hours, stirring occasionally; drain.
Melt the butter with 2 tbsp of the oil in a frying pan over a medium heat. Add the chicken pieces and sauté for about 5 minutes, stirring occasionally. Stir in the wine and cook a further few minutes until it evaporates.
Meanwhile, slice the *proscuitto* lengthwise into about 1 cm/^{1}/$_2$ in wide pieces. Roll the ham strips around the chicken pieces. Secure with a knot of the chives.
If you want to serve them hot, heat them in a 200°C/400°F/Gas 6 oven for about 5 minutes.
Arrange on a platter and serve.
Makes 18.

BOCCONCINI DI VERZA AL FOIS GRAS

Cabbage and Fois Gras Bites

Use the small and tender leaves from the centre of a head of savoy cabbage for this, or substitute Boston lettuce leaves.

18 cabbage leaves
360 g/12 oz fresh fois gras
2 cooking apples
30 g/1 oz/2 tbsp butter
Salt and pepper

Preheat the oven to 200°C/400°F/Gas 6. Bring a large pan of water to the boil. Add salt and the cabbage leaves and blanch for 1 minute. Drain, refresh under cold water and pat dry.
Slice the fois gras into 6. Peel, core and cut the apple into 18 slices.
Melt 1 tbsp of the butter in a frying pan. Add the apples and cook for a few minutes until tender. Melt the rest of the butter in another pan. Add the fois gras and cook over a high heat for 1 minute each side. Pat dry and cut each slice into 18 pieces. Add salt and pepper to taste.
Put a slice of apple and a piece of fois gras on each leaf, then roll to form a little package. Secure each with a cocktail stick (toothpick). Arrange the packages in an ovenproof dish and heat in the oven for about 5 minutes. Serve immediately, while still hot.
Makes 18.

BOCCONCINI DI SPECK

Speck Bites

Speck is becoming more and more popular in Italy. A speciality of the Alto Adige region, in north east of Italy, it is a variety of smoked ham. If you can't find it, use *prosciutto* or bacon, but bacon is fattier.

90 g/3 oz gorgonzola cheese
90 g/3 oz crescenza cheese or camembert, rind removed if necessary
9 walnuts
18 large prunes, stoned (pitted)
18 thin slices speck

In a bowl, cream both cheeses with a fork. Shell the walnuts and divide each in half. Insert the cheese mixture in the prunes and add half a walnut to each. Roll every prune in a slice of *speck* and secure with a cocktail stick (toothpick). Arrange on a dish and serve.
Makes 18.

UOVA SODE AI FUNGHI

Hard-cooked Eggs with Mushrooms

Hard-cooked eggs as appetizers were extremely popular in my parent's house when we had guests. The egg yolks, after being scooped out, can be mixed with a variety of ingredients such as canned tuna, smoked trout, chopped vegetables preserved in vinegar, ricotta cheese and herbs. This variation with mushrooms is particularly tasty if you use *porcini* mushrooms instead of button mushrooms.

6 eggs
210 g/7 oz fresh porcini mushrooms
90 g/3 oz/6 tbsp ricotta cheese
1 tbsp finely chopped fresh flat-leaf parsley
2 tbsp vin santo or dry sherry
Salt

Put the eggs in a large saucepan, cover with water and bring to the boil. Cook for 8 minutes, then drain and cool under cold water. Shell and cut the eggs in half lengthwise, then scoop out the yolks. Wipe the *porcini* with a cloth to clean, then chop finely.
Mix the mushrooms with the eggs yolks, ricotta, parsley, *vin santo* and a little salt. Transfer to a pastry bag with a fluted tip and pipe into the scooped out egg whites. Arrange on a platter and serve.
Makes 12.

Opposite page: Speck Bites

CROCCHETTE DI RISO

Rice Croquettes

My suggestion is to fill these with a piece of smoked provola but, in fact, any cheese such as fontina, mozzarella or emmenthal will do. Or you can use ham, sausage or sautéed chicken livers.

12 handfuls arborio rice
3 large eggs (U.S. extra large)
60 g/2 oz/¹/₂ cup Parmesan cheese, freshly grated
2 tbsp finely chopped fresh flat-leaf parsley
120 g/4 oz provola cheese, diced
120 g/4 oz/1 cup dry fine breadcrumbs
960 ml/32 fl oz/4 cups vegetable oil for deep-frying
Salt and pepper

Bring 960 ml/32 fl oz/4 cups water to the boil in a large saucepan. Add salt and the rice and boil for about 15 minutes until the water evaporates, without stirring. Let it cool completely.
Add the eggs, parmesan, parsley and pepper to taste to the rice. Form into walnut-sized balls. Press a piece of provola into each ball. Mould the rice around the provola so the cheese is enclosed. Place the breadcrumbs in a shallow bowl. Roll the balls in the breadcrumbs. Heat a large pan of oil to 180°C/350°F, or until a cube of bread turns golden brown in 1 minute. Add the croquettes and deep-fry for about 10 minutes until golden and crispy. Drain well on paper towels. Arrange on a platter and serve immediately, while still hot.
Makes 30.

CROCCHETTE DI PATATE

Potato Croquettes

In a small restaurant near Sorrento, these *croquettes* are served by the metre and they are so wonderful that a metre is the minimum you would eat. Very starchy white potatoes are the ones to use for this recipe.

1.2 kg/3 lb very starchy unpeeled potatoes
60 g/2 oz/4 tbsp unsalted butter
60 g/2 oz/¹/₂ cup freshly grated parmesan cheese
3 large eggs (U.S. extra large)
120 g/4 oz/1 cup plain (all-purpose) flour
120 g/4 oz/1 cup dry fine breadcrumbs
960 ml/32 fl oz/4 cups vegetable oil for deep-frying
Salt and pepper

Bring a large pan of water to the boil. Add salt and the unpeeled potatoes and boil until barely tender. Drain and peel while still hot, then pass them through a ricer. Stir in the butter, parmesan, 1 egg, salt and pepper to taste, stirring until well blended. Mould into cylinders about 5 cm/2 in long and 2.5 cm/1 in wide. Beat the remaining eggs in a deep dish. Roll the cylinders in the flour, then in the eggs and finally in the breadcrumbs to coat well.
Heat the oil in a frying pan to 180°C/350°F, or until a cube of bread turns golden brown in 1 minute. Add the croquettes and deep-fry for about 10 minutes until slightly golden and crispy. Drain well on paper towels. Arrange on a platter and serve immediately, while still very hot.
Makes 30.

PATATE CROCCANTI

Crisp Potato Slices

You can prepare these potatoes ahead of time, by keeping the slices in a bowl of water until it is time to cook them. They will release a little starch which makes them crisper once cooked. Dry them well. (This is a good trick to remember when you are frying potatoes.)

6 large, unpeeled baking potatoes
4 tbsp extra virgin olive oil
1 tbsp sweet paprika
6 tbsp balsamic vinegar
Salt

Preheat the oven to 200°C/400°F/Gas 6.
Scrub the potatoes, but do not peel them. Cut them lengthwise into paper-thin slices. Line a few baking sheets with parchment paper and arrange the potato slices in single layers. Brush them with the oil and sprinkle with salt. Roast in the oven for about 10 minutes, or until golden and crisp. Arrange the slices on a serving platter and sprinkle with the paprika. Serve warm or at room temperature, with a little bowl of balsamic vinegar for dipping.
Serves 6.

COSTOLETTINE IMPANATE

Small Fried Scaloppine

These are very popular at cocktail parties in Italy. For a vegetarian version, you can use vertically sliced courgettes (zucchini), fresh fennel bulbs, aubergines (eggplant) or artichokes. The scaloppine are usually about 4 cm/$1\frac{1}{2}$ in round and 0.2 cm/$\frac{1}{8}$ in thick. Cut them into three parts to obtain the correct bite-sized pieces.

18 veal scaloppine, thinly sliced
2 large eggs (U.S. extra large)
120 g/4 oz/1 cup fine dry breadcrumbs
2 tbsp finely chopped fresh sage leaves
2 tbsp finely chopped fresh rosemary needles
60 g/2 oz/4 tbsp unsalted butter
4 tbsp extra virgin olive oil
Salt

Cut the scaloppine into bite-size pieces as described above. Lightly beat the eggs in a soup bowl and place the breadcrumbs in another shallow bowl.
Add the herbs to the crumbs and mix well. Season the eggs with the salt.
Dip the scaloppine in the eggs and then in the breadcrumbs to coat well, shaking off any excess coating.
Melt the butter with oil in a heavy-based frying pan. Add the scaloppine and fry over a medium heat for about 2 minutes each side until crisp and golden. Remove with a slotted spoon and drain well on paper towels. Arrange on a platter and serve warm or at room temperature.
Serves 18.

ROTOLINI DI ZUCCHINE

Little Courgette (Zucchini) Rolls

Make sure you select very fresh and small courgettes (zucchini) for these small rolls because they are not cooked. If, however, you can only find larger courgettes that are not tender, grill (broil) them before filling.

6 small courgettes (zucchini)
210 g/7 oz canned tuna in oil, drained
180 g/6 oz/$\frac{3}{4}$ cup ricotta cheese
2 tbsp extra virgin olive oil
1 red or yellow (bell) pepper
1 tbsp capers in vinegar, drained

Slice the courgettes (zucchini) lengthwise, cutting off the tough ends. Place the tuna, ricotta and oil in a blender or food processor and blend until creamy.
Dice the pepper, discarding ends and seeds. Add the pepper to the tuna mixture and stir in the capers.
Spread the tuna mixture on top of the courgette (zucchini) slices. Roll them up and secure with cocktail sticks (toothpicks). Arrange upright on a platter so that the filling shows. Serve.
Makes 30.

ZUCCHINE FRITTE

Deep-fried Courgettes (Zucchini)

Some people prefer to fry courgettes (zucchini) in a batter, but I think they taste best just coated with flour. You will need quite fresh and not too large courgettes for this.

6 small courgettes (zucchini)
120 g/4 oz/1 cup plain (all-purpose) flour
960 ml/32 fl oz/4 cups vegetable oil for deep-frying
Salt

Cut off the courgette (zucchini) ends, then cut the flesh into long narrow strips. Sprinkle with salt, put in a colander and leave for about 1 hour until they are quite wet. Pat dry in paper towels. Put the courgette strips in a paper bag with the flour and shake the bag to coat well. Place them in the dried colander again and shake to eliminate any excess flour.
Heat the oil in a deep frying pan to 180°C/350°F, or until a cube of bread turns golden brown in 1 minute. Add the courgettes and fry for about 5 minutes until golden and crispy. Drain well on paper towels. Arrange on a platter and serve immediately, while still hot.
Serves 6.

ZUCCHINE RIPIENE AI FUNGHI

Courgettes (Zucchini) Filled with Porcini Mushrooms

You can make many variations on this dish, replacing the *porcini* mushrooms with finely chopped ham or *mortadella*, a speciality from Bologna, or *salame*.

1 handful dry porcini mushrooms
6 courgettes (zucchini)
1 handful fresh breadcrumbs
120 ml/4 fl oz/¹/₂ cup milk
1 egg
3 tbsp freshly grated parmesan cheese
2 tbsp extra virgin olive oil
Salt and pepper

Soak the *porcini* in a bowl of water for about 30 minutes. Drain, squeeze dry and chop. Preheat the oven to 180°C/350°F/Gas 4. Bring a large pan of water for the boil. Add salt and the courgettes (zucchini) and cook for about 5 minutes until almost tender; the exact time depends on the freshness of the courgettes. Soak the breadcrumbs in the milk for a few minutes, then squeeze dry.
Combine the breadcrumbs, mushrooms, egg, cheese and a little salt and pepper in a bowl. Cut the courgettes (zucchini) into 2.5 cm/1 in cylinders, discarding the ends. Scoop them out about half way through with a teaspoon to make a hollow. Fill with the bread and mushroom mixture. Brush an ovenproof dish with the oil, then arrange the courgette (zucchini) cups upright. Cook in the oven for about 20 minutes, or until the surface becomes slightly golden. Arrange on a platter and serve warm.
Makes 18.

ZUCCHINE RIPIENE DI PROSCIUTTO

Courgettes (Zucchini) Filled with Ham and Goats' Cheese

You can make many variations on the filling, substituting ricotta or Mayonnaise (page 177) for the goats' cheese and, of course, canned tuna for the ham. Small onions are also a good alternative to the courgettes.

6 very fresh medium-size courgettes (zucchini)
90 g/3 oz cooked ham, chopped
120 g/4 oz fresh goats' cheese
1 tbsp chopped fresh mint
2 tbsp extra virgin olive oil
Salt

Bring a large pan of water to the boil. Add salt and the courgettes (zucchini) and cook for about 5 minutes until still firm, but not crispy, depending on the freshness of the courgettes. Drain, refresh under cold running water and cut off the ends. Cut the courgettes crosswise into 2.5 cm/1 in pieces and use a teaspoon to hollow them out slightly. Beat the ham with the cheese, mint and olive oil. Transfer to a pastry bag fitted with a fluted tip and pipe into the courgette (zucchini) cups. Arrange on a platter and serve.
Makes 18.

SPIEDINI DI VERDURE ALLA GRIGLIA

Grilled (Broiled) Vegetable Skewers

Cherry tomatoes are becoming fashionable in Italy. I use them in pasta or rice dishes as well as preparations such as these skewers. To be grilled (broiled), however, they must be very firm. I think they are wonderful mixed with (bell) peppers, small onions, courgettes (zucchini) or other vegetables.

12 small onions
12 cherry tomatoes
1 (bell) pepper, possibly yellow, cored, seeded and diced
1 aubergine (eggplant), diced
2 small firm courgettes (zucchini), diced
3 tbsp extra virgin olive oil
Salt and pepper

Preheat the grill (broiler) to high. Alternate 2 onions, 2 tomatoes, 2 pieces of pepper, 2 pieces of aubergine (eggplant) and 2 pieces of courgette (zucchini) on 6 skewers. Place under a hot grill, turning them frequently, and brushing with the oil, for about 15 minutes. Sprinkle with salt and pepper to taste. Serve immediately, while still very hot.
Makes 6.

SPIEDINI DI PANCETTA E CIPOLLINE

Onion and Pancetta Skewers

The best onions for this recipe are the small and flat ones; baby round onions are usually tough. Unfortunately the flat ones only seem to be available in Italian markets. To make peeling them easy, blanch the onions for a couple of minutes in boiling water – the skins will then slip off.

30 small onions, blanched and peeled
15 pancetta slices, cut in half
12 bay leaves, cut in half
2 tbsp extra virgin olive oil

Preheat the grill (broiler). Roll the onions up in the *pancetta* slice, then alternate on 6 skewers with the bay leaves. Brush with the oil. Grill (broil) under a hot grill for about 20 minutes, turning them frequently, until the *pancetta* becomes golden and crisp. Arrange on a platter and serve immediately, while still hot.
Makes 6.

SPIEDINI DI MELANZANA

Aubergine (Eggplant) Skewers

My mother's home chef told me that there is no need to salt the aubergines (eggplants) to eliminate their bitter taste, because when they are fresh and very firm they can be cooked as they are. I find that aubergines with a long shape are the best kind for this recipe.

3 long aubergines (eggplants)
180 g/6 oz fresh goats' cheese
1 handful fresh basil, chopped
1 handful unroasted pine nuts
2 garlic cloves, finely chopped
120 g/4 oz pancetta or bacon rashers

Preheat the oven to 200°C/400°F/Gas 6, and preheat the grill (broiler). Slice the aubergines (eggplants) thinly lengthwise, discarding the tough ends. Place them under a hot grill for 2 minutes, turning once. Combine the cheese, basil, pine nuts and garlic until a soft cream forms. Spread the cream on top of the aubergine (eggplant) slices and roll them up. Wrap the pancetta slices around the outside and secure with a cocktail stick (toothpick).
Place in an ovenproof dish and cook in the oven for about 10 minutes, or until the *pancetta* becomes golden. Arrange on a platter and serve immediately.
Makes 18.

SALVIA FRITTA

Fried Sage

This is one of the favourite appetizers in my classes. We use fresh sage just picked from the garden. Not only are the leaves very tasty, they are also exceptionally large.

1 large egg (U.S. extra large)
75 g/2¹/₂ oz/¹/₂ cup plain (all-purpose) flour
960 ml/32 fl oz/4 cups vegetable oil for deep-frying
18 large sage leaves
Salt

Beat the egg with 60 ml/2 fl oz/¹/₄ cup water and salt to taste. Place the flour in a bowl and gradually add the egg mixture, beating with an electric mixer. Heat the oil in a deep frying pan to 180°C/350°F, or until a cube of bread turns golden brown in 1 minute. Dip the sage leaves in the batter. Add them to the oil and fry for 2 minutes until golden and crispy. Remove with a slotted spoon and drain on paper towels. Arrange on a platter and serve immediately, while still hot.
Makes 18.

SPIEDINI DI FRUTTA E FORMAGGIO

Little Cheese and Fruit Skewers

You can use other cheeses, such as aged goats' cheese, or sheep's milk cheese, and include pear, apple, mango or kiwi fruit on the skewers.

120 g/4 oz smoked provola cheese
120 g/4 oz fontina cheese
120 g/4 oz provolone cheese
18 strawberries
18 red or white grapes
4 unpeeled figs, quartered

Dice the cheese into bite-sized cubes. Alternate the cheese with the pieces of fruit on the skewers. Arrange on a platter and serve.
Makes 18.

SPIEDINI DI CAPRINI AL SESAMO

Goats' Cheese, Fig and Sesame Seed Skewers

A little unusual, but a very nice combination. The secret is to use figs that are not too ripe and to keep them in the refrigerator until the last moment.

300 g/10 oz fresh goats' cheese
2 tbsp balsamic vinegar
120 g /4 oz/³/₄ cups sesame seeds
6 figs

Mix the cheese with balsamic vinegar. Form into 18 bite-sized balls, rolling them in the sesame seeds to cover completely. Rinse the figs and slice them crosswise, discarding the ends. Alternate the cheese balls with the fig slices on 6 wooden skewers. Arrange on a platter and chill until ready to serve.
Makes 6.

Opposite page: Fried Sage

RAVIOLI AL FORNO RIPIENI DI PROSCIUTTO

Baked Ravioli with Ham and Ricotta

Traditionally *ravioli* are boiled, but I decided to try them baked, and the result was delicious. The filling can also include sautéed porcini mushrooms or sautéed and chopped chicken breasts.

For the dough:
240 g/8 oz/2 cups plain (all-purpose) flour
2 large eggs (U.S. extra large)
For the filling:
120g/4 oz cooked ham
120 g/4 oz/$\frac{1}{2}$ cup ricotta cheese
45 g/1$\frac{1}{2}$ oz/3 tbsp parmesan cheese, freshly grated

Preheat the oven to 180°C/350°F/Gas 4.
Heap the flour in a bowl and make a well in the centre. Break in the eggs. Using a fork, work the flour into the eggs until a dough is formed. Knead the dough on a lightly floured work surface for about 5 minutes until smooth and elastic. Cut the dough into 2 equal portions and, using a pasta machine, roll out the portions into very thin sheets; they should be about 10 cm/4 in wide.
To make the filling, finely chop the ham, then mix with the ricotta and parmesan cheese.
Place mounds of the filling at regularly spaced intervals along the edge of the pasta sheets, about 5 cm/2 in apart. Brush the edges of the dough with a little water and fold over the strips to cover the mounds of filling. Press the edges together to seal. Using a fluted pastry (biscuit) cutter, cut between the mounds to form squares. Transfer the squares on to a baking sheet covered with parchment paper. Bake in the oven for about 20 minutes, or until golden and crisp. Arrange on a platter and serve, preferably while still warm.
Makes 30.

LIMONI RIPIENI DI CREMA DI BACCALÀ

Lemons with Cream of Salt Cod

If you can't find salt cod, substitute poached salmon, boiled prawns (shrimp) or canned tuna.

300 g/10 oz salt cod fillets
2 large potatoes
6 tbsp double (heavy) cream
3 tbsp extra virgin olive oil
3 lemons
2 tbsp snipped fresh chives

Keep the salt cod covered with abundant water for 24 hours in a bowl, changing the water at least 6 times to remove all the salt. Remove any bones from the fillet. Transfer to a pan with enough water to cover. Bring to the boil and cook over a low heat for about 5 minutes. Drain well.
In another pan of salted water, boil the potatoes in their skins until tender, or easily pierced with a fork. Drain and peel when cool enough to handle.
Put the salt cod, potatoes, cream and oil in a food processor and blend until creamy. Cut the lemons into thick slices, discarding the ends. Just before serving, transfer the fish mixture to a pastry bag with a large tip and pipe the mixture on top of the lemon slices. Sprinkle with the chives. Arrange on a platter and serve.
Makes 18.

GNOCCHI DI RICOTTA

Ricotta Dumplings

These delicious ricotta gnocchi are a speciality of our restaurant chef, Massimo, who recently went for training at *Chez Panisse*, Alice Waters' famous restaurant in Berkeley, California. This dish can be served as an appetizer with drinks because the semolina coating will be crisp enough to allow the gnocchi to be picked up with fingers.

900 g/2 lb/3 cups ricotta cheese
150 g/5 oz/1¼ cups plain (all-purpose) flour
1 large egg (U.S. extra large)
90 g/3 oz. freshly grated parmesan cheese
Pinch grated nutmeg
240 g/8 oz/1²/₃ cups coarse semolina
Salt and pepper

Preheat the oven to 180°C/350°F/Gas 4. Put the ricotta in a bowl. Add the flour, egg, cheese, nutmeg, salt and pepper to taste, stirring until well blended. Using your hands, shape the mixture into walnut-sized balls, and roll them in the semolina to coat.
Bring a large pan of water to the boil. Add salt and the ricotta gnocchi, a few at a time. Remove with a slotted spoon as soon as they come to the surface and arrange in an ovenproof dish. Bake in the oven for about 20 minutes until a light crust forms. Arrange on a platter and serve hot or at room temperature.
Makes 30.

FRITTATINE ALLE ERBE

Small Frittatas with Herbs

Frittate can also easily be finger food if cooked until firm and cut into bite-size pieces. This is only one example of the endless possibilities – the filling can include chopped courgettes (zucchini), green beans, onions, canned tuna, aubergines (eggplants) or (bell) peppers.

1 kg/2¼ lb fresh spinach
6 large eggs (U.S. extra large)
60 g/2 oz/1 cup chopped mixed fresh herbs, such as flat-leaf parsley, dill, basil, marjoram, oregano and rocket (arugula)
1 tbsp extra virgin olive oil
6 radishes
1 small onion
Salt and pepper

Bring a large pan with a little water to the boil. Add the spinach leaves and cook for 2 minutes until just wilted. Drain well, squeeze to remove all the water and chop finely.
Beat the eggs in a large bowl. Add the spinach, herbs, salt and pepper to taste.
Heat the oil in a non-stick frying pan. Pour in the eggs and cook over a medium heat until the eggs have almost set. Turn the frittata over, sliding it on to a plate, then back into the pan. Cook the second side another couple of minutes until firmly set. Allow to cool completely, then cut into 2.5 cm/1 in squares. Slice the radishes and onions finely and arrange on top of the frittata squares as garnish. Arrange on a platter and serve.
Makes 30.

MOZZARELLA IN CARROZZA

Fried Mozzarella Sandwiches

This is a well known Neapolitan dish, perfect to be served as an antipasto. I usually use the small mozzarella called *bocconcini*, but the bigger size works just as well if you cut it into bite-size pieces.

6 small mozzarella (bocconcini)
36 slices bread, about 1 cm/^{1}/$_2$ in thick
120 g/4 oz/1 cup plain (all-purpose) flour
3 large eggs (U.S. extra large)
4 tbsp milk
960 ml/32 fl oz/4 cups vegetable oil for deep-frying
Salt

Slice each mozzarella into 1 cm/^{1}/$_2$ in thick slices. Using a pastry (biscuit) cutter, cut the bread the same size. Put a slice of mozzarella between 2 bread slices and press together. Coat these sandwiches well with the flour. Beat the eggs with the milk and a little salt in a shallow bowl. Put the sandwiches in the egg batter, rolling them around from time to time, until all the eggs have been absorbed.
Heat the oil in a deep frying pan to 180°C/350°F, or until a cube of bread turns golden brown in 1 minute. Working in batches, add as many sandwiches as will fit in a single layer and fry on both sides until golden and crispy; it will take a few minutes. Drain on paper towels and keep hot in a low oven. Arrange on a platter and serve immediately, while still hot.
Makes 18.

ROTOLINI DI VITELLO ALLA SALVIA

Veal Rolls with Sage and Prosciutto

These veal rolls are very popular and can also be served cold as appetizers, arranged on a dish with cocktail sticks (toothpicks). Usually, however, larger rolls are served bigger in size as a main dish, or on top of risotto.

600 g/20 oz veal scaloppine, sliced very thin
150 g/5 oz prosciutto
2 handfuls fresh sage leaves
15 g/^{1}/$_2$ oz/1 tbsp unsalted butter
2 tbsp extra virgin olive oil
120 ml/4 fl oz/1^1/$_2$ cup dry white wine
Salt and pepper

Cut the meat into thin 7.5 x 5 cm/3 x 2 in slices, then cut the *prosciutto* a little smaller. Top each piece of veal with a slice of ham and a sage leaf. Roll up and secure each roll with a wooden cocktail stick (toothpick). Heat the butter with the oil in a frying pan. Add the meat rolls and fry until slightly brown. Stir in the wine and salt and pepper to taste. Cover and cook over a low heat for about 40 minutes, turning the rolls from time to time and adding a little water to keep it moist. Drain and remove the cocktail sticks (toothpicks). Arrange on platter and serve warm or at room temperature.
Makes 18.

PINZIMONIO

Vegetables Dipped in Olive Oil

This is one of the best-known Tuscan antipasti and relies on very fresh vegetables and the best quality oil. The vegetables are arranged and a bowl of oil is provided for each guest to dip their vegetables into. Rampini, a terracotta maker in Gaiole, sells hand-painted bowls that my students love to buy.

1 fennel bulb
1 bunch white celery
2 carrots
1 red or yellow (bell) pepper
1 head red radicchio
1 artichoke
any other crunchy vegetable as desired
240 ml/8 fl oz/1 cup extra virgin olive oil
Salt and pepper

Rinse, trim and slice the vegetables lengthwise in strips or wedges. Arrange them in a serving bowl. Pour the oil into a smaller bowl and add salt and pepper to taste. Serve.
Serves 6.

PALLINE DI FORMAGGIO ALLE NOCCIOLE

Cheese Balls with Hazelnuts

Use different cheeses for a variety of flavours from the same recipe. Good alternatives for the goats' cheese are gorgonzola, camembert and brie, or even a grating cheese such as fontina, gruyère or emmenthal. The coating can also be varied with seeds such as cumin, cardamom or fennel.

300 g/10 oz/1¹/₄ cups ricotta cheese
300 g/10 oz fresh goats' cheese
120 g/4 oz/1 cup hazelnuts, toasted, skinned and finely chopped
1 tbsp sweet paprika

Beat the ricotta and goats' cheese together. Using your hand, form into walnut-sized balls, then roll them in the hazelnuts until well coated. Cover and chill until ready to serve. Sprinkle with the paprika, arrange on a platter and serve.
Makes 30.

CETRIOLI AL FORMAGGIO DI CAPRA

Cucumbers with Goats' Cheese

I find cucumbers quite refreshing, but their taste is not one everyone likes. If you find this so, substitute lightly boiled courgettes (zucchini).

300 g/10 oz fresh goats' cheese
3 tbsp extra virgin olive oil
1 tbsp finely chopped fresh mint
600 g/1¹/₄ lb cucumbers
Salt and pepper

In a bowl mix the cheese with the oil, mint and salt and pepper to taste. Cut off the ends of the cucumbers, then cut them in cylinders about 4 cm/1¹/₂ in long. Use a teaspoon to scoop out most of the seeds, creating a hollow.
Transfer the cheese to a pastry bag and pipe the mixture into the cucumbers. Arrange on a platter and serve.
Makes 18.

Opposite page: Vegetables Dipped in Olive Oil

PALLINE DI FORMAGGIO ALL'UVETTA

Cheese Balls with Raisins

The contrast between the saltiness of the cheese and the sweetness of the raisins is particularly interesting, and the Wilhelmina liqueur adds a nice touch to an unusual recipe. Wilhelmina is a pear liqueur and a speciality of Alto Adige. I particularly like the flavour. Sometimes the bottles are attached to trees so that a pear grows in the bottle. When the pear is ripe the bottle is filled with liqueur.

120 ml/4 fl oz/1 cup dry, very small dark raisins (currants)
120 ml/4 fl oz/1 cup Wilhelmina or grappa
90 g/3 oz creamy cheese, such as taleggio or camembert, rind removed if necessary

90 g/3 oz gorgonzola cheese
90 g/3 oz/6 tbsp ricotta cheese
90 g/3 oz mascarpone cheese

Put the raisins in a bowl, pour over the Wilhelmina and let stand for about 12 hours, stirring sometimes so that the raisins become soft. Drain the raisins and pat dry. Beat the taleggio, gorgonzola, ricotta and mascarpone cheese until well blended. Form into walnut-sized balls, then roll in the raisins to coat. Cover and chill for a couple of hours before arranging them on a platter and serving.
Makes 18.

FANTASIA DI FORMAGGI

Cheese Fantasy

Every coating ingredient here is just a suggestion – for variation try spices, chopped fresh herbs and sweet paprika.

180 g/6 oz provolone cheese in one thick slice
180 g/6 oz fontina cheese in one thick slice
180 g/6 oz scamorza cheese in one thick slice
45 g/1½ oz/3 tbsp unsalted butter at room temperature
For coating:
2 tsp chopped fresh flat-leaf parsley
2 tsp pine nuts
2 tsp sultanas (golden raisins)
2 tsp sesame seeds

Cut the cheeses into small rectangles about 2.5 x 1 cm/1 x ½ in. Cream the butter and spread on top of the cheese squares. Top the cheese with the different coating ingredients, pressing lightly with the palm of your hand. Refrigerate for at least 1 hour before serving. Arrange on a platter and serve.
Makes 30.

CAROTE ALLA CREMA DI RICOTTA

Carrots with Ricotta Cream

I also serve this creamy mixture as a dip with celery sticks, fennel bulbs, chicory (Belgian endive) leaves or strips of (bell) peppers.

6 medium carrots
240 g/8 oz/1 cup ricotta cheese
120 g/4 oz/½ cup plain yogurt
1 tsp grated fresh horseradish
1 tbsp finely chopped fresh flat-leaf parsley
Salt and pepper

Peel the carrots, then cut them into sticks. Put them in bowl filled with water, add a few ice cubes and keep in the refrigerator for a couple of hours to keep them crisp. Drain and dry in a cloth.
Combine the ricotta cheese with the yogurt, then stir in the horseradish, parsley and salt and pepper to taste. Transfer the dip to a serving bowl on a platter and surround with the carrot sticks.
Serves 6.

Opposite page: Cheese Balls with Raisins

TARTUFI CON PANCETTA

Truffles with Pancetta

When you want to really enjoy life, disregarding the cost of ingredients, try this delicacy. It was a must in autumn at my grandmother's castle of Monale near Asti in Piemonte. Black truffles are also a good substitute and they will be less expensive. If you are still worried about economy, however, you can try the commercially produced *scorzone* but it doesn't have the flavour of the genuine thing.

6 white truffles, about 30 g/1 oz each
6 slices pancetta, cut quite thin

Preheat the oven to 200°C/400°F/Gas 6. Clean the truffles by brushing the surface, but do not rinse them with water. If using *scorzone*, peel them. Wrap every truffle in a *pancetta* slice.
Place on a baking sheet and cook in the oven for about 10 minutes, or until the *pancetta* becomes crispy and slightly golden. Arrange on a platter and serve immediately, while still hot.
Makes 6.

TARTUFI DI PERE E FORMAGGIO

Cheese and Pear Truffles

Serve these truffles on a platter, or on top of cream crackers, or salted biscuits like the ones on page 92. If you serve them on crackers do not put them on top until the last minute because the biscuits will become soggy in the refrigerator.

300 g/10 oz gorgonzola cheese
300 g/10 oz/1¼ cups mascarpone cheese
2 Bosch pears, not too ripe
Juice of 1 lemon
120 g/4 oz/1 cup freshly grated parmesan cheese

Mix the gorgonzola and mascarpone cheese together until well blended. Peel the pears, then core and cut the flesh into small dice. Sprinkle with the juice and combine with the two cheeses. Using a spoon, form the mixture into walnut-sized balls then roll them in the parmesan to coat well. Arrange on a platter and refrigerate for a couple of hours before serving.
Makes 30.

POMODORI IN COSTOLETTA

Tomatoes in a Bread Crust

The best tomatoes for this recipe are the ones that are still green in autumn with no hope of ripening and in danger of being lost. I use them in many ways, such as jams, chutneys and pasta sauces, or fried as in this recipe.

6 green tomatoes
120 g/4 oz/1 cup fine dry breadcrumbs
2 large eggs (U.S. extra large)
1 tbsp dried oregano
30 g/1 oz/2 tbsp unsalted butter
30 g/1 oz/4 tbsp extra virgin olive oil
Salt and pepper

Slice the tomatoes about 0.5 cm/¼ in thick. Place in a colander, sprinkle with salt and let them drain for about 1 hour. Pat dry in a cloth.
Put the breadcrumbs in a shallow dish and beat the eggs in another shallow dish. Add the oregano to the breadcrumbs with a little pepper to taste. Coat the tomato slices with the egg and then the breadcrumbs. In a large frying pan melt the butter with the oil. Add the tomato slices, a few at a time and fry for about 3 minutes on each side, or until slightly golden and crispy. Arrange on a platter and serve while still hot.
Serves 6.

SCODELLINE DI POMODORI AL TONNO

Little Tomato Cups with Tuna

Plum tomatoes are perfect for the recipe, but otherwise medium-sized salad tomatoes can be substituted. You can also replace the tuna fish with boiled peas or beans such as *canellini*.

6 plum tomatoes
210 g/7 oz canned tuna fish in oil or brine, drained
6 tbsp Mayonnaise (page 177), or good-quality commercial
1 tbsp capers in vinegar, drained and chopped

2 anchovy fillets in oil, drained
1 tbsp chopped fresh flat-leaf parsley

Cut the tomatoes in half lengthwise and scoop out the seeds. Flake the tuna and combine it with the mayonnaise, capers and anchovies.
Fill the tomatoes with the tuna mixture and sprinkle with the parsley. Arrange on a platter and serve.
Serves 6.

SFOGLIATELLE DI PARMIGIANO

Parmesan Crisps

These crisps are delicious served simply with a glass of dry white wine, but they are really a treat dipped in balsamic vinegar, as we sometimes do in my cooking classes. They can be eaten at room temperature or warm, and will stay crisp for a couple of days in an airtight container. It is always best to buy parmesan and grate it yourself.

300 g/10 oz freshly grated parmesan cheese

Preheat the oven to 180°C/350°F/Gas 4. Cover a baking sheet with parchment paper and sprinkle the parmesan into mounds. Use a small knife to flatten the mounds into 5 cm/2 in rounds that are almost paper thin. Cook in the oven for about 10 minutes, or until golden and crispy. Remove and place on a wire cooling rack. Serve immediately or allow to cool completely.
Makes 18.

CAPPELLE DI FUNGHI AI GAMBERETTI

Mushroom Caps with Prawns (Shrimp)

For this recipe, I like to use button mushroom caps because it is easy to find a selection that are the same size. The stems can be saved and used to flavour a soup or for making a risotto.

18 medium-size button mushroom caps
210 g/7 oz uncooked prawns (shrimp), peeled and deveined
120 g/4 oz/¹/₂ cup mascarpone cheese
120 g/4 oz/¹/₂ cup fresh thyme or tarragon
Juice of 1 lemon
Salt

Wipe the mushroom caps with a cloth but do not rinse with water. Bring a pan of water to the boil. Add the prawns (shrimps) and boil for 2 minutes. Drain and leave to cool completely then chop finely.
Stir together the mascarpone, prawns, thyme or tarragon, lemon juice and salt to taste. Transfer the mixture to a pastry bag fitted with a fluted tip and pipe into the mushroom caps. Cover and chill until ready to serve. Arrange on a platter and serve.
Makes 18.

GAMBERETTI MARINATI

Marinated Prawns (Shrimp)

Buy prawns (shrimp) with the tail still attached, so it is easy to pick them up. Otherwise, just serve them with coloured cocktail sticks (toothpicks) or on top of paper-thin lemon wedges.

18 uncooked prawns (shrimp), as big as possible
2 lemons
1 orange
2 tbsp extra virgin olive oil
3 drops hot pepper sauce
Salt

Rinse the prawns (shrimps) and place in a bowl. Squeeze the juice from the lemons. Grate the zest from the orange and set aside, then squeeze the juice. Pour the juices over the prawns and let them marinate for a couple of hours in the refrigerator.
Combine the oil, hot pepper sauce and a little salt. Drain the prawns and arrange on a serving platter. Sprinkle with the oil mixture and garnish with orange zest. Serve.
Makes 18.

Opposite page: Parmesan Crisps

GRISSINI, FOCACCE, PIZZETTE

MOST OF THESE ANTIPASTI ARE BAKED, AND IN MY EXPERIENCE THEY ARE THE FIRST TO DISAPPEAR FROM THE TABLE.

Grissini are those little bread sticks wrapped in cellophane you find on the table of practically every Italian restaurant. Home-baked grissini, especially when seasoned with a herb, are an entirely different experience. The hand-rolled, irregular shape also makes them more interesting. They are especially attractive on a buffet table, maybe with a transparently thin slice of *prosciutto* wrapped around the top.

Focacce are flat breads and each region of Italy has its special kind, preferred topping and often its own local name. Some *focacce*, usually ones eaten as a midday snack to stave off hunger, are sweet. I guarantee these savory *focacce* will stimulate the appetite of your guests.

Pizzette are individual-size *pizze*. They constitute a tasty and welcome addition to any party. *Pizzette* can be thin or thick, round or square and dressed in dozens of ways. If you fold one over and stuff something delicious in between, you will have a little *calzone*. I have also included a recipe that is a family favourite for fried savoury pizza dough, as well as fried bread seasoned with herbs.

GRISSINI AI SEMI DI PAPAVERO

Poppy Seed Grissini

These breadsticks make an enjoyable appetizer with a glass of white wine. You can enrich them by wrapping Parma ham (*prosciutto*) around the top slices. Or use *speck*, a smoked ham speciality from Alto Adige.

30 g/1 oz/2 tbsp fresh yeast
240 ml/8 fl oz/1 cup lukewarm water
120 g/4 oz/1 cup plain (all-purpose) flour
180 g/6 oz/1^1/2 cups wholemeal (wholewheat) flour
40 g/1^1/2 oz/^{1}/4 cup coarse semolina
5 tbsp extra virgin olive oil
40 g/1^1/2 oz/^{1}/4 cup poppy seeds
Salt

Dissolve the yeast in the water for about 10 minutes. Combine the flours, semolina, 4 tablespoons of the oil and salt to taste in a large bowl. Start pouring in the yeast mixture a little at a time, mixing with a fork in a circular motion, until everything is well combined. Transfer the dough to a work surface and knead with the heel of your palms until it becomes smooth and elastic (about 10 minutes). Shape into a ball. Oil a bowl with the rest of the oil and place the dough in it. Cover with cling film (plastic wrap) and let it rise for about 1 hour, or until doubled in volume.
Preheat the oven to 200°C/400°F/Gas 6. Sprinkle the work surface with the poppy seeds. Knock back (punch down) the risen dough and place on a floured work surface. Flatten with a rolling pin and roll into a rectangle of about 1 cm/^{1}/2 in thick. Cut the dough into 1 cm/^{1}/2 in thick strips, shape into sticks and roll in the poppy seeds.
Cover a baking sheet with parchment paper and arrange the breadsticks on top. Let rise for about 10 minutes. Bake in the oven for about 20 minutes, or until lightly golden and crisp. Let cool and serve.
Makes 18.

BISCOTTI SALATI ALLA SALVIA

Sage Biscuits (Crackers)

These *biscotti* are made with bread dough and poked with a fork so that they do not rise, and baked twice to make them crisp. *Biscotti* will remain crisp if stored in an airtight container for about 2 weeks.

30 g/1 oz/2 tbsp fresh yeast
240 ml/8 fl oz/1 cup lukewarm water
360 g/12 oz/3 cups plain (all-purpose) flour
6 tbsp extra virgin olive oil
6 tbsp finely chopped fresh sage
Salt

Dissolve the yeast in the water for about 10 minutes. Put the flour in a bowl. Pour in the yeast mixture and half the oil. Add the sage and mix with a fork in a circular motion until everything is well blended. Transfer the dough to a work surface and knead with the heel of your palms until smooth and elastic. Shape into a ball. Put the dough in a floured bowl and cover with cling film (plastic wrap) and let rise for about 1 hour until doubled in volume.
Preheat the oven to 200°C/400°F/Gas 6. Knock back (punch down) the dough on a floured work surface. Flatten with a rolling pin and roll into a rectangle about 0.2 cm/^{1}/8 in thick.
Cover the base of a baking sheet with parchment paper, then transfer the dough rectangle on to it. Using a knife, score 5 cm/2 in squares into the dough and prick with a fork. Brush the top with the rest of the oil and sprinkle with salt. Bake in the oven for about 15 minutes. Remove from the oven and separate the biscuits (crackers) completely with a knife. Return to the oven for a further 5 minutes. Let cool on a wire rack completely before serving.
Makes 30.

Opposite page: Poppy Seed Grissini

PIADINE AL PROSCIUTTO

Flatbreads with Ham

Here's a very traditional antipasto from Emilia Romagna, often eaten folded in half and filled with *prosciutto*, cooked ham, salami or *mortadella*. *Piadine* are usually baked on a *testo*, a terracotta stone heated with embers, but a heavy cast-iron frying pan over a gas flame works just as well.

360 g/12 oz/3 cups plain (all-purpose) flour
120 ml/4 fl oz/¹/₂ cup water
1 tsp baking soda
120 ml/4 fl oz/¹/₂ cup milk
210 g/7 oz prosciutto, thinly sliced
Salt

Combine the flour, baking soda and milk with the water. Add a little salt to taste. Transfer the dough to a work surface and knead for about 10 minutes with the heel of your palms until very smooth. Form the dough into 6 walnut-sized balls, then flatten them to 0.2 cm/¹/₈ in thick.
Heat a large cast-iron frying pan over a high heat. Add the *piadine* and cook for about 1 minute each side, or until brown spots form. Cook in batches if necessary. Let them cool a bit, then top them with *prosciutto*. Fold in half and serve warm or at room temperature.
Makes 6.

PANE FRITTO ALLE ERBE

Fried Bread with Herbs

A nice variation of the Piedmontese *Bagna cauda*, this is perfect to serve for a small number of guests. You will need a Swiss fondue set, or simply put a small heatproof pot in the middle of the table with a candle underneath, because the oil has to remain hot all the time to fry the bread.

30 g/1 oz/2 tbsp fresh yeast
120 ml/4 fl oz/¹/₂ cup lukewarm water
360 g/12 oz/3 cups plain (all-purpose) flour
60 g/2 oz/4 tbsp unsalted butter
120 ml/4 fl oz/¹/₂ cup lukewarm milk
1 tbsp rosemary needles
1 tbsp chopped fresh sage leaves
1 tbsp chopped garlic
480 ml/14 fl oz/2 cups extra virgin olive oil
Salt and pepper

Use the yeast, flour, butter, milk and the water to make a pizza dough following the recipe for *Pasta per Pizza* (page 182), melting the butter in the milk and water.
Meanwhile, preheat the oven to 200°C/400°F/Gas 6. Brush a 32.5 x 7.5 cm/13 x 9 in cake tin (pan) with oil.
Knock back (punch down) the dough. Place it in the cake tin, pressing the dough into the corners. Bake in the oven for about 30 minutes, or until well puffed and slightly golden. Let cool on a wire rack, then turn out. Slice the bread and divide each slice into 3 parts. Place the rosemary, sage, garlic and oil in a pot over a medium heat and heat to 180°C/350°F, or until a cube of bread browns in 1 minute. Place the pot over a candle in the middle of the table. Each person will spear a piece of bread and fry for a few minutes until golden and crisp before eating.
Makes 36.

FOCACCINE CON ZUCCHINE E PATATE

Small Focaccias with Courgettes (Zucchini) and Potatoes

Usually the difference between pizza and *focaccia* is that pizza is topped with tomatoes and other ingredients while *focaccia* is baked without tomatoes. But, of course, there are exceptions – in Naples, for example, where a pizza without tomatoes is still called *pizza bianca* (white pizza). Sometimes *focaccia* is called *schiacciata*, as in Tuscany.

30 g/1 oz/2 tbsp fresh yeast
240 ml/8 fl oz/1 cup lukewarm water
360 g/12 oz/3 cups plain (all-purpose) flour
2 courgettes (zucchini)
1 large potato
3 tbsp extra virgin olive oil
2 tbsp chopped fresh basil leaves
Salt and pepper

Use the yeast, flour, salt and the water to make a pizza dough, following the recipe for *Pasta per Pizza* (page 182).
Preheat the oven to 200°C/400F/Gas 6. Thinly slice the courgettes (zucchini) and peel and slice the potato thickly. Bring a large pan of water to the boil. Add the potatoes and when the water returns to the boil, add the courgettes and boil for a further few minutes. Drain and mix with the olive oil, then sprinkle with salt and pepper to taste. Knock back (punch down) the dough and place on a floured work surface. Form the dough into walnut-sized balls then flatten them to 0.2 cm/¹/₈ in thick. Transfer the dough to a baking dish covered with parchment paper. Arrange the courgettes and potato slices on top, alternating them in concentric circles. Leave to rise for 10 minutes. Bake in the oven for about 20 minutes, or until a golden crust forms. Transfer to a serving platter. Sprinkle with basil and serve while still warm.
Makes 6.

FOCACCINE ALLE ERBE

Small Focaccias with Herbs

So many fresh herbs are now available in supermarkets, but if you can't find any substitute dried herbs, such as oregano, mint or tarragon. You can also use spices, such as fennel, cumin or coriander seeds.

30 g/1 oz/2 tbsp fresh yeast
240 ml/8 fl oz/1 cup lukewarm water
360 g/12 oz/3 cups plain (all-purpose) flour
1 tbsp very finely chopped fresh sage
1 tbsp very finely chopped fresh rosemary needles
1 tbsp fresh thyme leaves
1 tbsp very finely chopped garlic
3 tbsp extra virgin olive oil
Salt and pepper

Use the yeast, flour, salt and the water to make a pizza dough, following the recipe for *Pasta per Pizza* (page 182).
Preheat the oven to 200°C/400°F/Gas 6. Combine the sage, rosemary, thyme and garlic with the oil and salt and pepper to taste in a small bowl. Knock back (punch down) the dough and place on a floured work surface. Form the dough into 6 walnut-sized balls, then flatten them to 0.2 cm/¹/₈ in thick. Transfer them to a baking sheet covered with parchment paper. Brush the tops with the herb and garlic mixture. Bake in the oven for about 20 minutes, or until a golden crust forms. Transfer to a serving platter. Serve hot or at room temperature.
Makes 6.

FOCACCE DI CECI AL ROSMARINO

Chick-pea Focaccias with Rosemary

Chick-pea flour is usually available in health food stores or from Italian speciality delicatessens; in Indian food stores it is sold as *besal* flour. This recipe is also very good if you replace the chick-pea flour with chestnut flour, and, of course, you can also use rosemary with sage or even replace the rosemary with dry mint.

3 large eggs (U.S. extra large)
90 g/3 oz/³/₄ cup chick-pea flour
1 tbsp extra virgin olive oil
240 ml/8 fl oz/1 cup milk
2 tbsp finely chopped fresh rosemary needles
15 g/¹/₂ oz/1 tbsp unsalted butter
Salt

Whisk the eggs in a bowl. Add the flour a little at a time, always whisking. Incorporate the oil, then the milk and rosemary. Add salt to taste.
Melt very little butter in a 17.5 cm/7 in non-stick frying pan over a medium heat. Pour in just enough of the mixture to cover the bottom, about 0.2 cm/¹/₈ in thick. Cook for a couple of minutes until set. Slide on to a plate, flip over, return to the pan and cook the other side for just 1 minute. Remove from the pan and keep warm while you make 5 more. Serve immediately, while still very warm.
Makes 6.

CIACCINO ALL'AGLIO

Thin Focaccia with Garlic

This Tuscan speciality is rolled very thin and sprayed with water to make the crust very crispy. (Spraying is usually important to achieve a crisp crust on any bread.)

30 g/1 oz/2 tbsp fresh yeast
240 ml/8 fl oz/1 cup lukewarm water
360 g/12 oz/3 cups plain (all-purpose) flour
6 tbsp extra virgin olive oil
3 tbsp finely chopped garlic
3 tbsp finely chopped pancetta
Salt and pepper

Use the yeast, flour, salt and the water to make a pizza dough, following the recipe for *Pasta per Pizza* (page 182), adding the oil with the yeast mixture. Preheat the oven to 200°C/400°F/Gas 6. Knock back (punch down) the dough and place on a floured work surface. Flatten with a rolling pin and roll into a paper-thin rectangle. Cover the base of a baking sheet with parchment paper, then transfer the dough rectangle on to it. Sprinkle with garlic and *pancetta* and salt and pepper to taste. Prick with a fork. Bake in the oven for about 20 minutes, spraying twice with water, until a golden, crisp crust forms. Leave to cool on a wire rack and break into pieces with the hands before serving.
Serves 6.

Opposite page: Chick-pea Focaccias with Rosemary

CALZONI ALLE CIPOLLE

Small Calzoni Filled with Onions

These are easier than pizzas to eat with fingers, because the filling is enclosed. The anchovies can be replaced with fresh goats' cheese or black olives, such as Gaeta or Kalamata, stoned (pitted) and cut in half. A Neapolitan friend of mine often holds buffets and her *calzoni* filled in various ways are always a success.

30 g/1 oz/2 tbsp fresh yeast
240 ml/8 fl oz/1 cup lukewarm water
360 g/12 oz/3 cups plain (all-purpose) flour
3 tbsp extra virgin olive oil
3 red onions
6 anchovy fillets in oil, drained
Salt and pepper

Use the yeast, flour, salt and the water to make a pizza dough, following the recipe for *Pasta per Pizza* (page 182), adding half the oil with the yeast mixture. Meanwhile, preheat the oven to 200°C/400°F/Gas 6. Slice the onions thinly and chop the anchovies. Heat the remaining oil in a frying pan. Add the onions and anchovies and cook, covered, over a low heat, for about 30 minutes, until the onions are tender, occasionally adding water if necessary. Remove from the heat, sprinkle with salt and pepper to taste and let cool. Knock back (punch down) the dough and place on a floured work surface. Flatten with a rolling pin and roll into a large round about 0.2 cm/¹/₈ in thick. Using a 5 cm/2 in biscuit cutter, cut out about 18 circles. Arrange the onions on half of a dough circle, then fold over the other half to enclose the filling. Pinch the edges to seal. Repeat with the remaining dough. Cover a baking sheet with parchment paper and arrange the *calzoni* on top. Bake in the oven for about 20 minutes, or until golden. Transfer to a serving platter. Serve warm.
Makes 18.

CALZONI CON SPINACI

Calzoni with Spinach

The spinach leaves can be replaced with Swiss chard, beetroot leaves or even broccoli if preferred. Sometimes I use savoy cabbage for a stronger taste.

30 g/1 oz/2 tbsp fresh yeast
240 ml/8 fl oz/1 cup lukewarm water
360 g/12 oz/3 cups plain (all-purpose) flour
1 kg/2¹/₄ lb fresh spinach leaves
3 tbsp extra virgin olive oil
210 g/7 oz fresh goats' cheese
Salt and pepper

Use the yeast, flour, salt and the water to make a pizza dough, following the recipe for *Pasta per Pizza* (page 182), adding half the oil with the yeast mixture. Meanwhile, preheat the oven to 200°C/400°F/Gas 6. Rinse the spinach in several changes of cold water, do not remove the stems. Blanch in boiling salted water for about 2 minutes. Drain well. Heat the remaining oil in a large frying pan. Add the spinach and sauté for about 5 minutes, stirring occasionally. Add pepper to taste. Let cool slightly, then mix with the goats' cheese.
Knock back (punch down) the dough and place on a floured work surface. Flatten with a rolling pin and roll out until 0.2 cm/¹/₈ in thick. Using a 15 cm/6 in pastry (biscuit) cutter cut out 6 rounds. Arrange one-sixth of the spinach and cheese mixture on half of a dough circle, then fold over the other half to enclose. Pinch the edge to seal. Repeat with the remaining dough and filling.
Cover a baking sheet with parchment paper and place the *calzoni* on top. Bake in the oven for about 20 minutes, or until golden and crusty. Arrange on a platter. Serve immediately, while still hot.
Makes 6.

CALZONI ALLO STRACCHINO E TARTUFI

Calzoni with Stracchino and White Truffles

Sometimes I make this recipe with my basic pizza dough. For a more elegant antipasto, I layer pancakes (crêpes) like the one on page 104 with this filling.

30 g/1 oz/2 tbsp fresh yeast
210 ml/7 fl oz/³/₄ cup lukewarm water
360 g/12 oz/3 cups plain (all-purpose) flour
300 g/10 oz stracchino cheese or camembert or brie, rind removed if necessary
120 g/4 oz/¹/₂ cup ricotta cheese
60 g/2 oz/4 tbsp freshly grated parmesan cheese
1 white truffle, about 30 g/1 oz (optional)
Salt

Use the yeast, flour, salt and the water to make a pizza dough, following the recipe *Pasta per Pizza* (page 182) Meanwhile, preheat the oven to 200°C/400°F/Gas 6. Combine the stracchino, ricotta and parmesan cheese, then grate the white truffle on top and delicately stir. Knock back (punch down) the dough and place on a floured surface. Divide into 6 pieces, and roll out each until 0.2 cm/¹/₈ in thick. Arrange one-sixth of the cheese and truffle mixture on half of a dough circle, then fold over the other half to enclose. Punch the edge to seal. Repeat with the remaining dough and filling. Cover a baking sheet with parchment paper and arrange the *calzoni* on top. Bake for about 20 minutes or until golden and crusty. Serve immediately while still very warm.
Makes 6.

PICCOLI CALZONI ALLA PANCETTA

Small Calzoni with Pancetta

These *calzoni* are just as excellent if you use bacon instead of *pancetta*. The smoky taste is very appealing and goes well with a glass of white wine.

30 g/1 oz/2 tbsp fresh yeast
240 ml/8 fl oz/1 cup lukewarm water
360 g/12 oz/3 cups plain (all-purpose) flour
3 tbsp extra virgin olive oil
240 g/8 oz smoked pancetta or bacon, finely diced
Salt and pepper

Use the yeast, flour, salt and the water to make a pizza dough, following the recipe for *Pasta per Pizza* (page 182). Heat the oil in a frying pan over a medium heat. Add the *pancetta* and fry until crisp and golden. Drain and leave to cool; discard the excess fat.
Preheat the oven to 200°C/400°F/Gas 6.
Knock back (punch down) the dough and place on a floured surface. Form the dough into 6 walnut-sized balls, then flatten them to 0.2 cm/¹/₈ in thick. Place one-sixth of the *pancetta* on half of a dough circle, then fold over to enclose. Punch the edge to seal.
Repeat with the remaining dough and filling.
Cover a baking sheet with parchment paper and place the calzoni on top. Bake for about 20 minutes or until golden and crusty. Arrange on a platter and serve immediately while still warm.
Makes 6.

PIZZETTE DI PATATE

Small Potato Pizzas

It is essential to make these pizzas with quite starchy potatoes. I use the ones with a white flesh, the same good-quality potatoes I use to make *gnocchi*.

500 g/1 lb unpeeled starchy potatoes
180 g/6 oz/1½ cups plain (all-purpose) flour
120 ml/4 fl oz/½ cup milk
1 large egg (U.S. extra large)
4 tbsp extra virgin olive oil
6 garlic cloves, finely chopped
2 tbsp finely chopped flat-leaf parsley
Salt

Preheat the oven to 200°C/400°F/Gas 6.
Boil the potatoes in their skins until tender. Drain, and when cool enough to handle, peel and mash while still warm. Add the flour, milk, egg and salt to taste, stirring in a circular motion until a dough forms.
Place on a floured work surface and roll into a log about 5 cm/2 in thick. Cut into slices about 0.5 cm/¼ in thick then pat to smooth with your hands. Cover a baking sheet with parchment paper and place the small pizzas on top. Bake in the oven for about 20 minutes, turning them over a couple of times until golden.
Meanwhile heat the oil in a frying pan. Add the garlic and fry until barely golden, then stir in the parsley. Arrange the pizzas on a serving platter and sprinkle with the oil and garlic mixture. Serve immediately, while still very hot.
Makes 18.

PIZZETTE AL TALEGGIO

Small Pizzas with Fontina and Porcini Mushrooms

These small pizzas can be round, or even square, by just making a big rectangular form and cutting it into small squares before covering with the cheese and cooking.

30 g/1 oz/2 tbsp fresh yeast
240 ml/8 fl oz/1 cup lukewarm water
360 g/12 oz/3 cups plain (all-purpose) flour
210 g/7 oz creamy cheese, such as taleggio or camembert, rind removed if necessary
3 tbsp double (heavy) cream
210 g/7 oz fresh porcini mushrooms
3 tbsp extra virgin olive oil
1 garlic clove, finely chopped
1 tbsp finely chopped fresh flat-leaf parsley
Salt

Use the yeast, flour, salt and the water to make a pizza dough, following the recipe *Pasta per Pizza* (page 182) Meanwhile, preheat the oven to 200°C/400°F/Gas 6.
Beat the cheese with the cream until soft. Wipe the mushrooms with a cloth but do not rinse, then slice thinly. Heat the oil in a frying pan with the garlic over a medium heat, stirring until the garlic is barely golden. Add the mushrooms and sauté for about 3 minutes, stirring with a wooden spoon from time to time. Add the parsley and salt to taste. Knock back (punch down) the dough and place on a floured work surface. Form into 6 walnut-sized balls, then flatten them to 0.2 cm/⅛ in thick.
Transfer to a baking sheet covered with parchment paper. Distribute the cheese on top of the pizzas and top with the mushrooms. Bake in the oven for about 20 minutes, or until the crusts are slightly golden. Arrange on a platter and serve immediately, while still hot.
Makes 6.

PIZZETTE DI PATATE AL PARMAGIANO

Small Potato Pizzas with Parmesan Cheese

More delicate than pizzas made with the usual dough, these are a Neapolitan speciality, derivating from the popular *gatto' di patate*, or potato cake. Be careful to use very starchy potatoes or the same thing will happen to you that happened to me the first time I tried them, years ago. The pizzas melted in the oven and I had to quickly arrange something different for my guests.

1 kg/2 lb unpeeled starchy potatoes
2 large eggs (U.S. extra large)
60 g/2 oz freshly grated parmesan cheese
15 g/^{1}/$_2$ oz/1 tbsp unsalted butter
Salt and pepper

Preheat the oven to 180°C/350°F/Gas 4.
Cover the potatoes with cold water, add salt and bring to the boil. Cook until tender, then drain, and when cold enough to handle, peel and mash. Let cool a little, then beat in the eggs, cheese and pepper to taste. Butter a rectangular 33 x 25 cm/13 x 10 in cake tin and spread the potato mixture 0.5 cm/^{1}/$_4$ in thick. Bake for about 10 minutes until barely golden. Use a 5 cm/2 in pastry (biscuit) cutter to cut out 18 circles. Use a palette knife (metal spatula) to transfer the little pizzas to a baking sheet. Bake for a further 10 minutes until a little crispy. Arrange on a serving platter and serve warm or at room temperature.
Makes 18.

BIGNE' AL FORMAGGIO

Cheese Puffs

These puffs are also delicious if filled with a creamed mixture of ricotta cheese and ham, or even better with shaved white truffle mixed with a creamy cheese, or gorgonzola cheese mixed with mascarpone cheese. You just need to cut off the puff top, fill the centre and replace the top.

120 g/4 oz/1 stick unsalted butter
Pinch grated nutmeg
480 ml/16 fl oz/2 cups water
240 oz/8 oz/2 cups plain (all-purpose) flour
150 g/5 oz/1^1/$_4$ cups freshly grated parmesan cheese
4 large eggs (U.S. extra large)
Salt

Preheat the oven to 180°C/350°F/Gas 4.
Bring a large pan of water to the boil. Add the butter, nutmeg and salt to taste. When the butter melts, remove the pan from the heat and add all the flour at once, stirring vigorously with a wooden spoon. Return the pan to a medium heat, stirring until the dough leaves the side of the pan and forms into a ball.
Remove from heat and leave to cool almost completely. Add the eggs and beat in, one by one, adding each egg only after the previous one has been incorporated. When the dough is smooth add the parmesan.
Cover a baking sheet with parchment paper. Using a teaspoon, drop walnut-sized balls on to it, not too close together. Bake in the oven for about 20 minutes, or until puffy and slightly golden. Arrange on a serving platter and serve warm or at room temperature. Or fill them before serving with the suggested fillings in the introduction.
Makes 36.

PANZEROTTI

Fried Pizza Dough

This is a typical recipe from southern Italy. It is also popular in other parts of the country with different names and sometimes different fillings, such as soft cheeses, chopped ham or a piece of sausage. Sometimes the *panzerotti* are not filled, but eaten just as they are.

30 g/1 oz/2 tbsp fresh yeast
240 ml/8 fl oz/1 cup lukewarm water
360 g/12 oz/3 cups plain (all-purpose) flour
9 anchovy fillets in oil, drained and halved
960 ml/32 fl oz/4 cups vegetable oil for deep-frying
Salt

Use the yeast, flour, salt and the water to make a pizza dough, following the recipe for *Pasta per Pizza* (page 182).
Knock back (punch down) the dough and place on a floured work surface. Form into 8 walnut-sized balls, then fill each one with an anchovy fillet. Flatten to about 0.5 cm/¼ in thick.
Heat the oil in a large frying pan until about 180°C/350°F or until a cube of bread browns in 1 minute. Fry the *panzerotti* a couple at a time until very puffy and barely golden. To make them puffy, spoon some of the oil over the tops while frying.
Drain well on a paper towel. Serve immediately while still very hot.
Makes 18.

GNOCCHI FRITTI AL FORMAGGIO

Fried Gnocchi with Cheese

A northern version of *panzerotti*, I have to prepare these for my son Guido every time he comes back from college.

30 g/1 oz/2 tbsp fresh yeast
120 ml/4 fl oz/½ cup lukewarm water
120 ml/4 fl oz/½ cup milk
360 g/12 oz/3 cups plain (all-purpose) flour
960 ml/32 fl oz/4 cups vegetable oil for deep-frying
240 g/8 oz soft creamy cheese such as stracchino, camembert or brie, rind removed if necessary
Salt

Use the yeast, milk, flour, salt and the water to make a pizza dough, following the recipe for *Pasta per Pizza* (page 182).
Knock back (punch down) the dough and place on a floured work surface. Form into walnut-sized balls, then flatten to 0.2 cm/⅛ in thick.
Meanwhile, heat the oil in a frying pan to 180°C/350°F or until a cube of bread browns in 1 minute. Fry the *gnocchi* a few at a time until puffy and barely golden. To make them puffy, spoon some of the oil over the tops while frying. Drain well on a paper towel. Cut each in half and fill with the cheese.
Serve them as warm as possible.
Makes 18.

Opposite page: Fried Pizza Dough

CRESPELLE AI FUNGHI

Pancakes (Crêpes) with Porcini Mushrooms

This classical Italian filling for pancakes (crêpes) has numerous variations. My wonderful chef, Hatidza, might fill them with *béchamel* sauce with ham or ricotta cheese, with sautéed prawns (shrimp) or scallops, according to the mood of the day.

For the pancakes (crêpes):
3 large eggs (U.S. extra large)
120 g/4 oz/1 cup plain (all-purpose) flour
240 ml/8 fl oz/1 cup milk
15 g/¹/₂ oz/1 tbsp unsalted butter
For the filling:
15 g/¹/₂ oz/1 tbsp unsalted butter
2 tbsp plain (all-purpose) flour
480 ml/16 fl oz/2 cups milk
90 g/3 oz cooked ham, chopped
90 g/3 oz/¹/₂ cup freshly grated parmesan cheese
1 handful dry porcini mushrooms, soaked in water for at least
30 minutes, squeezed and chopped
Fresh chive stems
Salt and pepper

To make the pancakes (crêpes), beat the eggs in a bowl. Add the flour, a little at a time, then incorporate the milk and salt and pepper to taste.

Melt very little butter in a 22 cm/9 in non-stick frying pan over a medium heat. Pour in enough of the mixture to cover the bottom of the pan with a veil and cook for a couple of minutes until set. Remove from the pan and continue to make pancakes (crêpes) until all the mixture is used.

Preheat the oven to 180°C/350°F/Gas 4.

To make the filling, melt the butter in a saucepan for about 2 minutes. Add the flour and stir in the milk, a little at a time, to make a white sauce. Off the heat, stir in the ham, cheese and mushrooms, adding salt and pepper to taste.

Put 1 tbsp of the filling in the centre of each pancake (crêpe) then lift up the edges of the pancake (crêpe) and tie into a bundle with a chive, with the edge opening like a flower.

Cover the bottom of a baking sheet with parchment paper and place the pancake bundles on top. Cook in the oven for about 20 minutes, or until golden.

Arrange on a platter and serve immediately, while still hot.

Makes 18.

PART III
FORK FOOD

Most of the recipes in this section are for the type of antipasto you might want to serve on its own at a more formal dinner or party. Many of them are also perfect as a single course for a light luncheon or supper.

In Italian homes we almost never serve food already prepared on individual plates. That is considered restaurant-style service. Instead we arrange the food simply and elegantly on a platter, which might be served by a waiter or simply passed around by the guests. I sometimes make an exception to this custom of etiquette when I serve these fork food antipasti dishes. They can be attractively prepared on individual plates beforehand and, depending on the occasion, placed at the table before your guests take their seats, which simplifies serving and gets the meal off to an expeditious start.

TORTE, FRITTATE, TIMBALLI

THESE ARE ALL MOULDED DISHES. TRADITIONALLY MANY OF THESE RECIPES WERE SERVED AS A *PIATTO DI MEZZO, ENTREMETS* BETWEEN COURSES OF A MEAL. THIS CUSTOM ENDURED INTO THE FIRST DECADES OF THE TWENTIETH CENTURY. MANY OLD RECIPE BOOKS EXPLAIN THAT RECIPES FOR ANTIPASTI AND *PIATTI DI MEZZO* ARE SUITABLE FOR EITHER COURSE.

Torte are savoury pies and for centuries they were very elaborate creations, filled with all sorts of wonderful ingredients. My contemporary interpretation of this old and elegant tradition is more streamlined, without any sacrifices to flavour.

Frittate is the Italian version of an omelet, which I have explained in the section of antipasto types, makes a delicious dish especially for summer buffets, since it can be served at room temperature. I present the entire round *frittate* on a platter, cut into wedges. For a summer luncheon you might want to make these the main course. Serve two or three types accompanied by a green salad. Remember to turn out *frittate* while they are still moist in the centre.

Timballi are perhaps the most elegant of the moulded dishes. They are not difficult to make after a little experience and they are so delicious that I am sure you will find them well worth the effort.

108

TORTA DI GORGONZOLA CON LE PERE

Gorgonzola Tart with Pears

When I have a more elegant lunch or dinner party I prepare this tart with puff pastry, but more simply I use the basic shortcrust (pie crust) pastry.

240 g/8 oz/2 cups plain (all-purpose) flour
120 g/4 oz/1 stick unsalted butter, in small pieces
1 large egg yolk (U.S. extra large)
2 tbsp milk
210 g/7 oz gorgonzola cheese
210 g/7 oz/³/₄ cup plus 2 tbsp mascarpone cheese
3 Bosch pears
Juice of 1 lemon
3 tbsp chopped walnuts

Use the flour, butter, egg yolk and milk to make shortcrust (pie crust) pastry, following the recipe for *Pasta Frolla* (page 182).
Preheat the oven to 180°C/350°F/Gas 4.
Roll out the pastry (dough) and line a 23 cm/9 in flan tin (tart pan) with a removeable bottom. Prick the pastry with a fork. Bake in the oven for about 30 minutes, or until slightly golden. Remove from the oven and let cool. Beat both cheeses together. Peel, core and thinly slice the pears, then sprinkle with the lemon. Spread over the baked tart shell. Add the pear slices and sprinkle with the walnuts. Arrange on a platter and serve.
Makes 6–8 slices.

TORTA DI BIGNÉ AI FUNGHI

Choux Ring with Porcini Mushrooms

I like to make several variations to this filling, such as replacing the *porcini* mushrooms with button or *shittake*, or adding a light white sauce (page 177). You can also try ricotta cheese with cooked spinach or sautéed potatoes, or fried onions mixed with a goats' cheese.

120 g/4 oz/1 stick unsalted butter
240 ml/8 fl oz/1 cup water
120 g/4 oz/1 cup plain (all-purpose) flour
4 large eggs (U.S. extra large)
3 tbsp extra virgin olive oil
300 g/10 oz fresh porcini mushrooms, wiped clean and sliced
120 g/4 oz cooked ham, chopped
120 g/4 oz/1 cup Parmesan cheese, freshly grated
Salt and pepper

Preheat the oven to 180°C/350°F/Gas 4.
Bring a large pan with the water to the boil. Add the butter and salt to taste. When the butter melts, remove the pan from the heat and add the flour all at once, stirring vigorously with a wooden spoon. Return the pan to a medium heat and beat until the dough leaves the side of the pan and forms a ball. Remove from the heat and leave to cool almost completely. Stir in the eggs, one at a time, adding each egg only after the previous one has been incorporated.
Cover a baking sheet with parchment paper. Use a spoon to drop rounds of the dough in a 23 cm/9 in circle. Bake in the oven for about 30 minutes, or until puffed and tripled in size; keep the oven door slightly open with a wooden spatula while cooking for the best results.
Meanwhile, heat the oil in a frying pan. Add the mushrooms and sauté for about 3 minutes over a medium heat. Add salt to taste and let cool. Stir in the ham and the cheese; set aside.
When the choux ring is baked, leave it to cool, then cut off the top. Transfer to a serving platter and fill with the mushroom mixture. Replace the top and serve at room temperature, or reheat for 15 minutes before serving.
Makes 6–8 slices.

TORTA DI MOZZARELLA E POMODORO

Mozzarella and Tomato Pudding

This very simple but delicious antipasto is an elegant and rich savoury bread pudding. It is important to make a thick tomato sauce and add it at the last minute.

30 g/1 oz/2 tbsp unsalted butter, melted
12 bread slices, about 1 cm/^{1}/$_2$ in thick
4 large eggs (U.S. extra large)
480 ml/16 fl oz/2 cups milk
300 g/10 oz mozzarella cheese
6 anchovy fillets in oil, drained
1 tbsp dry oregano
240 ml/8 fl oz/1 cup Tomato Sauce (page 178)
Salt and pepper

Preheat the oven to 180°C/375°F/Gas 4.
Use the butter to grease an ovenproof dish and arrange the bread slices in 2 layers, breaking them when necessary. Add the remaining butter. Beat the eggs and milk with salt and pepper to taste. Pour on top of the bread, then set aside for a couple of hours so that all the liquid is absorbed by the bread.
Slice the mozzarella cheese and arrange it on top of the bread. Cover with the anchovies and sprinkle with the oregano, then dot with the tomato sauce. Bake in the oven for about 40 minutes, or until puffed up and golden. Serve immediately, while still piping hot.
Makes 6–8 slices.

TORTA DI RICOTTA E PROVOLONE

Ricotta and Provolone Tart

This is a very southern Italian antipasto which is wonderful warm or cool. It is also perfect for brunches or picnics, combining the saltiness of the cheeses with the sweetness of the crust.

480 g/16 oz/4 cups plain (all-purpose) flour
240 g/8 oz/2 sticks unsalted butter, in small pieces
2 large egg yolks plus 2 whole large eggs (U.S. extra large)
120 g/4 oz/^{1}/$_2$ cup plus 2 tbsp granulated sugar
4 tbsp milk
240 g/8 oz/1 cup ricotta cheese
120 g/4 oz/1 cup freshly grated provolone cheese
90 g/3 oz prosciutto, julienned

Use the flour, butter, egg yolks, sugar and milk to make shortcrust (pie crust) pastry, following the recipe for *Pasta Frolla* (page 182), adding the sugar to the flour.
Preheat the oven to 180°C/350°F/Gas 4.
Divide the pastry into 2 portions, one a little larger than the second. Roll out the large portion with a rolling pin and line a buttered 23 cm/9 in flan tin (tart pan) with a removeable bottom. Mix together the ricotta cheese, provolone cheese, *prosciutto* and the whole eggs. Fill the tart with the mixture and level the surface. Roll out the second portion of pastry and put on top to cover. Cut away any excess pastry and prick the surface with a fork to let the steam evaporate. Bake in the oven for about 40 minutes, or until the top is slightly golden. Remove from the pan, slide on to a serving platter and serve warm or at room temperature.
Makes 6–8 slices.

TORTINO DI PATATE ALLE UOVA

Potato Cake with Eggs

This is a Piedmontese speciality from my grandmother's house that, in season, can be enriched by a *grattatina* of truffles (sliced white truffles) instead of the anchovies.

1 kg/2 lb unpeeled boiling potatoes
120 g/4 oz/1 stick unsalted butter
120 ml/4 fl oz/¹/₂ cup milk
120 g/4 oz freshly grated parmesan cheese
2 whole large eggs plus 6 large yolks (U.S. extra large)
12 paper-thin slices fontina cheese
12 anchovy fillets in oil, drained
Salt and pepper

Put the potatoes in a large saucepan, cover with water and bring to the boil. Boil for about 30 minutes until tender, then drain. When cool enough to handle, peel and mash while still hot. Leave in the pan and beat in half the butter, the milk and parmesan and heat over a low heat for about 10 minutes, stirring all the time with a wooden spoon. Add salt and pepper to taste. Leave to cool completely, then add 2 whole eggs, beating them well.
Meanwhile, preheat the oven to 180°C/350°F/Gas 4.
Butter a baking dish and spoon the potato mixture into it. Smooth with a knife and make 6 indentations, large enough to hold the egg yolks. Place a slice of fontina in each indentation, dotting the rest of the butter on top. Cook in the oven for about 20 minutes, or until barely golden. Fill the indentations with the egg yolks and cross each yolk with 2 anchovy fillets. Top with the rest of the fontina slices. Cook for a further 5 minutes, or until the fontina starts to melt, but the yolks remain runny. Serve immediately.
Makes 6–8 slices.

TORTA DI BROCCOLI E FORMAGGIO

Broccoli and Cheese Tart

For this tart you only use the broccoli florets, but the stems can be used in soups or puréed and added to mashed potatoes for extra taste. I think, whatever you use them for, the stems should always be peeled before using.

240 g/8 oz/2 cups plain (all-purpose) flour, plus 2 tbsp for dusting the flan tin (tart pan)
120 g/4 oz/1 stick unsalted butter
1 large egg yolk plus 2 large whole eggs (U.S. extra large)
2 tbsp milk
300 g/10 oz broccoli florets
150 g/5 oz fontina cheese
120 ml/4 fl oz/¹/₂ cup double (heavy) cream
Pinch grated nutmeg
Salt and pepper

Use the flour, butter, egg yolk and milk to make shortcrust (pie crust) pastry, following the recipe for *Pasta Frolla* (page 182).
Roll out the pastry until 0.2 cm/¹/₈ in thick, then use to line a buttered and dusted 23 cm/9 in flan tin (tart pan) with a removeable bottom. Keep in refrigerator until required.
Preheat the oven to 180°C/350°F/Gas 4.
Bring a large pan of water to the boil. Add salt and the broccoli florets and blanch for 1 minute. Drain. Dice the fontina. Beat the eggs with the cream, then add the nutmeg and salt and pepper to taste. Fill the tart case with the broccoli florets, cover with the fontina and pour the egg mixture on top. Bake in the oven for about 40 minutes, or until the surface becomes slightly golden. Remove from the tin (pan) and transfer to a serving platter. Serve warm.
Makes 6–8 slices.

TORTA DI PATATE ALLA SALSICCIA

Potato Cake with Sausages

I usually use Italian sweet sausages for this cake, but the neapolitan ones with hot pepper flakes will do; it is a matter of individual taste. Or you can replace the sausages altogether with chopped pancetta or bacon.

1 kg/2 lb unpeeled boiling potatoes
30 g/1 oz/2 tbsp unsalted butter
90 g/3 oz/²/₃ cup freshly grated fontina cheese
4 large eggs (U.S. extra large)
2 tbsp extra virgin olive oil
480 g/1 lb/3 cups sweet onions, sliced
120 ml/4 fl oz/¹/₂ cup double (heavy) cream
60 g/2 oz/¹/₂ cup dry fine breadcrumbs
210 g/7 oz/sweet Italian sausages, casings removed and crumbled

Boil the potatoes in their skins for about 40 minutes until tender. Drain well. When cool enough to handle, peel and purée with a ricer while still warm. Stir in half of the butter and the cheese, then leave to cool completely. Add 2 of the eggs.
Heat the oil in a large frying pan over a medium heat. Add the onions and sauté for about 10 minutes, stirring often until golden. Transfer them to a bowl and stir in the cream. Leave to cool, then add the remaining 2 eggs.
Meanwhile, preheat the oven to 180°C/350°F/Gas 4. Coat a 25cm/10 in flan tin (tart pan) with a removeable bottom with the remaining butter and the breadcrumbs. Add the potato mixture and spread, smoothing the surface with a knife. Pour the onion mixture on top and dot with the sausage. Bake for about 40 minutes, or until the top is golden. Let rest a few minutes, then remove from the tin and transfer to a serving platter. Serve warm.
Serves 6.

TORTA DI POLENTA ALLE CIPOLLE

Polenta Cake with Onion Cream

Polenta, undoubtedly of modest origins, has now assumed an elegance and is becoming more and more popular. This antipasto can also be a main course, and with a bit of imagination you will be able to use it in many variations.

1 kg/2 lb onions
30 g/1 oz/2 tbsp unsalted butter
2 tbsp extra virgin olive oil
Pinch grated nutmeg
210 g/7 oz fontina or asiago cheese, diced
240 g/8 oz/2 cups coarse polenta (yellow cornmeal)
1.5 litres/48 fl oz/6 cups water
Salt

Peel and slice the onions. Melt the butter with the oil in a large frying pan over a low heat. Add the onions and cook them, covered, for about 2 hours, until almost melted; if necessary, add water a little at a time to keep moist. Off the heat, stir in the nutmeg and the cheese.
Bring the water to the boil. Add salt and the polenta, a little at a time, whisking continuously. Cover and let cook for about 10 minutes.
Wet a 2 litre/64 fl oz mould of any shape with a little water and pour in half the polenta. Add all the onion mixture, then cover with the rest of polenta.
To serve, invert on to a serving platter and remove the mould. Serve immediately or, set it aside for a few hours and reheat in the mould in the oven at 180°C/350°F/Gas 4 for about 20 minutes before unmoulding and serving.
Serves 6.

TORTA DI FICHI E FORMAGGIO DI CAPRA

Fig and Goats' Cheese Tart

The best figs are usually the smallest, green or purple. Figs are ideal to combine with salted food, such as the goats' cheese in this recipe. They are also excellent with roasted lamb or pork and very popular with *prosciutto*.

340 g/12 oz/3 cups plain (all-purpose) flour
120 g/4 oz/1 stick unsalted butter, in small pieces
1 large egg yolk plus 2 whole large eggs (U.S. extra large)
1 tbsp milk
240 g/8 oz fresh goats' cheese
240 g/8 oz/1 cup ricotta cheese
6 figs
Pepper

Use the flour, butter, egg yolk and milk to make shortcrust (pie crust) pastry, following the recipe for *Pasta Frolla* (page 182).
Preheat the oven to 180°C/350°F/Gas 4.
Roll out the pastry until 0.2 cm/¹/₈ in thick, then use to line a 25 cm/10 in flan tin (tart pan) with a removeable bottom. Beat the 2 whole eggs, then beat in the goats' and ricotta cheeses and pepper to taste. Pour into the lined flan tin (tart pan), smoothing the surface with a knife.
Bake in the oven for about 30 minutes.
Meanwhile, peel and quarter the figs. After 30 minutes baking, arrange the figs on the cheese tart and bake for a further 10 minutes, or until the crust becomes golden. Leave to cool slightly on a wire rack.
Remove the tart from the tin and slide it on to a serving platter. Serve at room temperature.
Makes 10–12 slices.

TORTINO DI PATATE

Potato Cake

Similar to the Swiss *rösti*, but with a very Italian touch that comes from the chopped rosemary, this is also delicious topped with a soft, creamy cheese, such as stracchino, camembert or brie.

6 large potatoes
2 tbsp finely chopped rosemary needles
3 tbsp extra virigin olive oil
Salt and pepper

Peel and grate the potatoes. Mix them with the rosemary and salt and pepper to taste. Heat half the oil in a large frying pan. Add the potatoes and press them down firmly. Cover with a lid, not tightly, and cook over a low heat for about 10 minutes, shaking the pan from time to time. Carefully slide the potato cake on to the lid. Pour the rest of the oil into the pan and let the potato cake slide back into the pan. Cook on the other side for a further 10 minutes until potatoes are golden and crusty. Slide on to a platter and serve immediately, while still quite hot.
Serves 6.

Opposite page: Fig and Goats' Cheese Tart

TORTA DI FRITTATE

Frittata Tart

This is a very tasty presentation that can be varied in many ways by including grilled aubergines (eggplants) with courgettes (zucchini), slices of ham or thin slices of fontina or asiago cheese.

6 large eggs (U.S. extra large)
3 tbsp extra virgin olive oil
2 fairly large, round aubergines (eggplants)
15 g/^{1}/$_2$ oz/1 tbsp unsalted butter for buttering the dish
240 ml/8 fl oz/1 cup White Sauce (page 177)
500 g/1 lb cherry tomatoes
Salt and pepper

Preheat the oven to 180°C/350°F/Gas 4.
Beat the eggs separately with salt and pepper to taste.
Heat ^{1}/$_2$ tbsp of the oil in a 20 cm/8 in non-stick frying pan over a medium heat. Add 1 egg and cook until almost set. Using a palette knife (metal spatula), turn the thin *frittata* over and cook on the other side for about 45 seconds. Slide out of the pan and leave to cool. Prepare the other 5 eggs the same way and leave them to cool.
Slice the aubergines (eggplants) crosswide about 0.5 cm/^{1}/$_2$ in thick. Grill the slices for about 1 minute until tender then sprinkle with a little salt.
Butter a round 20 cm/8 in ovenproof dish and arrange the first *frittata* on the bottom. Spread with some white sauce and cover with a couple of aubergine slices. Top with the second *frittata* and continue layering until all the *frittate* are used. Spread with the rest of the white sauce and surround with the cherry tomatoes. Cook in the oven for about 20 minutes, or until hot. Serve immediately.
Serves 6.

'TRIPPA' DI FRITTATA

'Tripe' Frittata

This is a very particular 'tripe' people will not refuse, and it is also one of my dearest remembrance of childhood. You can serve it with a meat ragu or a tomato sauce like the one on page 178.

6 very large eggs (U.S. extra large)
3 tbsp extra virgin olive oil
480 ml/16 fl oz/2 cups Meat Sauce (page 178)
90 g/3 oz/6 tbsp freshly grated parmesan cheese
Salt and pepper

Beat the eggs separately with a little salt and pepper.
Heat ^{1}/$_2$ tbsp of the oil in a 23 cm/9 in non-stick frying pan over a medium heat. Add 1 egg and fry until almost set. Using a palette knife (metal spatula), turn the thin *frittate* over and cook on the other side for about 45 seconds. Slide out of the pan on to a dish and leave to cool. Prepare the other 5 eggs in the same way and leave them all to cool.
Roll up the thin *frittate* on a work surface. Then slice them crosswise into stripes about 1 cm/^{1}/$_2$ in thick. Meanwhile, reheat the *ragú* in a large saucepan. Add the *frittata* strips, cover and simmer over a medium heat for about 2 minutes, or until hot. Pour on to a serving platter and sprinkle with the parmesan cheese. Serve very warm.
Serves 6.

SFOGLIATA DI ZUCCHINE

Puff Pastry with Courgettes (Zucchini)

Although you can now buy quite decent commercial puff pastry, I like to make it at home. It takes only a little time and expertise to know the correct temperature and learn the correct consistency.

300 g/10 oz Puff Pastry (page 180), or good-quality commercial puff pastry
1 small onion
6 small courgettes (zucchini)
3 tbsp extra virgin olive oil
210 g/7 oz mozzarella cheese
1 handful fresh mint leaves
2 large eggs (U.S. extra large)
60 g/2 oz/^{1}/$_2$ cup freshly grated hard cheese, such as parmesan, fontina or pecorino
Salt and pepper

Preheat the oven to 190°C/375°F/Gas 5. Roll out the puff pastry into a circle large enough to line a 23 cm/9 in flan tin (tart pan); when using puff pastry you do not need to butter the tin. Slice the onion and courgettes (zucchini).
Heat the olive oil in a frying pan over a medium heat. Add the onion and courgettes and sauté for about 10 minutes, stirring occasionally with a wooden spoon. Add salt and pepper to taste.
Meanwhile, slice the mozzarella cheese. Off the heat, stir the cheese into the courgettes. Pour this mixture into the flan tin (tart pan) and sprinkle with the mint. Beat the eggs in a bowl, then pour them over the courgettes and cover with the grated parmesan, pecorino or fontina. Bake in the oven for about 40 minutes, or until golden on top. Leave to set for a few minutes. Remove from the tin and slide on to a serving platter. Serve immediately, while still warm.
Serves 6.

SFOGLIATA DI RADICCHIO

Radicchio in Puff Pastry

You can vary this recipe endlessly by replacing the radicchio with chicory (Belgian endive), cauliflower, broccoli or beetroot leaves.

60 g/2 oz/scant ^{1}/$_2$ cup raisins
300 g/10 oz red radicchio
3 tbsp extra virgin olive oil
3 anchovy fillets in oil, drained
300 g/10 oz Puff Pastry (page 180), or good-quality commercial puff pastry
90 g/3 oz/generous ^{1}/$_2$ cup black (ripe) olives, stoned (pitted)
Salt and pepper

Cover the raisins with water and soak for about 30 minutes until plump.
Preheat the oven to 180°C/350°F/Gas 4.
Halve the radicchio. Heat the oil in a frying pan over a medium heat. Add the radicchio and fry for about 5 minutes, or until wilted. Leave to cool. Meanwhile, drain the raisins. Chop the anchovies.
Roll out the puff pastry into a circle large enough to line a 25 cm/10 in flan tin (tart pan). Fill with the radicchio, then sprinkle with the raisins, anchovies and olives. Bake in the oven for about 40 minutes, or until the pastry is golden. Remove from the pan and slide on to a platter. Serve warm or at room temperature.
Serves 6.

FRITTATA RIPIENA ARROTOLATA

Filled Rolled Frittata

Another popular, elegant dish I recall eating many times in my parents' home. The filling can be sautéed spinach and ricotta for a vegetarian version.

6 large eggs (U.S. extra large)
3 tbsp extra virgin olive oil
240 ml/8 fl oz/1 cup White Sauce (page 177)
60 g/2 oz/¹/₂ cup freshly grated parmesan cheese
60 g/2 oz/4 tbsp unsalted butter, softened
210 g/7 oz cooked ham, sliced paper thin

Beat the eggs with salt and pepper to taste. Heat half the oil in a 30cm/12 in non-stick frying pan. Pour in half the egg mixture and cook until almost set. Slide the *frittata* on to a plate, then slide it back into the pan to cook the second side for about 45 seconds. Use the remaining eggs and oil to make a second *frittata*. Combine the white sauce with the parmesan cheese and butter. Spread the sauce on one side of each frittata, then cover with the ham slices. Roll up each to form 2 cylinders, then wrap tightly in cling film (plastic wrap). Refrigerate for at least 2 hours. Unwrap the *frittate* and slice about 1 cm/¹/₂ in thick. Arrange the slices overlapping on a serving platter. Serve at room temperature.
Serves 6.

STRUDEL DI PATATE E CAPRINO

Potato and Goats' Cheese Strudel

In this recipe I teach you how to make the real filo pastry dough, which almost no one does anymore, instead of buying the frozen variety. Take a little time to try making it – it is worthwhile and not so difficult, as I demonstrate in my cooking classes.

500 g/1 lb/4 cups plain (all-purpose) flour, plus extra
120 g/4 oz/1 cup for working and flouring the tin
360 ml/12 fl oz/1¹/₂ cups water
3 tbsp extra virgin olive oil
6 potatoes
1 large onion
210 g/7 oz fresh goats' cheese
30 g/1 oz/1 tbsp unsalted butter for buttering the tin
Salt

In a large bowl, whisk the flour with the water and a little salt with a fork until all the liquid is absorbed. Squeeze the dough with your hands until a soft and smooth dough forms. Sprinkle with a little flour, arrange in a bowl and cover with cling film (plastic wrap) and leave to rest for about 20 minutes at room temperature.

Roll out the dough with a floured rolling pin on a large table covered with a floured cloth into a 50 cm/20 in circle. Brush with 3 tbsp of the oil, entirely covering the surface. Leave to rest again for about 10 minutes.

Meanwhile, peel the potatoes and the onion. Use a grater to julienne both into a bowl. Add salt to taste and the cheese, mixing until well combined.

Preheat the oven to 180°C/350°F/Gas 4.

Put your hands under the dough and pull it all around until it becomes completely transparent: it will be at least triple the size of the initial circle. Spoon the potato and cheese mixture on the dough in a long row along one side. Roll up the dough with the help of the tablecloth: by pulling up the cloth the dough will roll. Enclose the filling completely in a long cylinder. Butter and flour a 27.5 cm/11 in flat tin (tart pan). Starting from the centre, roll the cylinder in a coil until the bottom of the tin (pan) is covered. Bake in the oven for about 50 minutes, or until the surface becomes slightly golden. Invert the strudel on to a serving platter and serve warm.
Serves 6.

Opposite page: Filled Rolled Frittata

FRITTATA SOFFIATA AI CARCIOFI

Artichoke Frittata Soufflé

This is an elegant way of presenting a frittata, and, of course, you can replace the artichokes with broccoli or courgettes (zucchini). In summer, this is delicious made with cherry tomatoes, which are not fried but just added raw.

1 tbsp extra virgin olive oil for coating the baking dish
6 artichokes
Juice of 1 lemon
120 g/4 oz/1 cup plain (all-purpose) flour
960 ml/32 fl oz/4 cups vegetable oil for deep-frying
6 large eggs (U.S. extra large)
Salt and pepper

Preheat the oven to 180°C/350°F/Gas 4. Brush a 30 cm/12 in soufflé dish with the oil; set aside. Clean the artichokes, discarding tough leaves and choke; drop them in a bowl with water and the lemon juice as they are prepared to prevent discolouring. When they are all prepared, pat dry and pass them in the flour to coat well.

Meanwhile, heat the oil in a large frying pan to 180°C/350°F, or until a cube of bread browns in 1 minute. Fry the artichokes for about 5 minutes until golden. Drain on paper towels. Separate the egg yolks from the whites. Beat the yolks with salt and pepper to taste. Beat the whites in another bowl until puffy and stiff. Fold the yolks into the whites. Arrange the artichokes in the prepared dish and cover with the eggs mixture. Cook for about 20 minutes until golden and puffy. Serve immediately, straight from the dish.

Serves 6.

CANNELLONI DI FRITTATA AL PROSCIUTTO E PROVOLONE

Frittata Cannelloni with Ham and Provolone Cheese

I also like to make many variations on this recipe, replacing the ham and provolone with salami and fontina or mozzarella, and *prosciutto*, ricotta cheese and cherry tomatoes

6 large eggs (U.S. extra large)
3 tbsp extra virgin olive oil
210 g/7 oz cooked ham, diced
210 g/7 oz provolone cheese, diced
30 g/1 oz/2 tbsp unsalted butter
90 g/3 oz/6 tbsp freshly grated parmesan cheese

Preheat the oven to 180°C/350°F/Gas 4.
Beat each egg separately with a little salt and pepper. Heat $1/2$ tbsp of the oil in a 20 cm/8 in non-stick frying pan over a medium heat. Add 1 of the eggs and cook until almost set. Using a palette knife (metal spatula), turn the thin *frittata* over and cook on the other side for about 45 seconds. Slide out of the pan and leave to cool. Prepare the other 5 eggs in the same way and leave them to cool.
Arrange the ham and provolone cheese on top of each frittata. Roll them up to form cylinders like cannelloni. Butter an ovenproof dish with half the butter and arrange the *frittata cannelloni* in it, distributing the rest of the butter on top. Sprinkle with the parmesan cheese. Cook in the oven for about 20 minutes, or until hot. Serve them immediately.

Serves 6.

FRITTATA DI PATATE E ACCIUGHE

Anchovy and Potato Frittata

This *frittata* can also be served at room temperature, and is wonderful to take along on picnics. If you like, replace the anchovies with canned tuna.

3 large baking potatoes
1 onion
5 tbsp extra virgin olive oil
60 g/2 oz/$\frac{1}{2}$ cup black olives, stoned (pitted)
60 g/2 oz/4 tbsp capers in vinegar, drained
6 large eggs (U.S. extra large)
1 tbsp dry oregano
6 anchovy fillets in oil, drained and chopped
Salt and pepper

Peel and slice the potatoes and the onion. Heat 4 tbsp of the oil in a 28 cm/11 in frying pan over medium heat. Add the potatoes and onion and cook for about 15 minutes until almost golden, stirring frequently with a wooden spoon. Let cool slightly, then stir in the olives and capers.
Beat the eggs in a large bowl with salt and pepper to taste. Add the oregano, anchovies and the cooled potatoes.
Heat the rest of the oil in a large non-stick frying pan over medium heat. Pour the egg mixture into it and cook for about 5 minutes on one side until almost set.
Slide out of the pan on to a plate, then slide the *frittata* back into the pan to cook the second side for just a couple of minutes. Transfer to a serving platter. Serve warm or at room temperature.
Serves 6.

FRITTATA DI MOZZARELLA E POMODORO

Tomato and Mozzarella Frittata

In Italy, *frittate* are extremely popular for homely dinners, and are always cooked on the hob (top of the stove) so they remain juicy in the centre – *frittata* cooked in the oven is always too dry.

6 large eggs (U.S. extra large)
3 tbsp double (heavy) cream
45 g/1$\frac{1}{2}$ oz/3 tbsp freshly grated parmesan cheese
2 tbsp extra virgin olive oil
300 g/10 oz very ripe, plum tomatoes, peeled and diced
210 g/7 oz mozzarella cheese, sliced
60 g/2 oz rocket (arugula)
Salt and pepper

Beat the eggs in a bowl with the cream and parmesan cheese. Add salt and pepper to taste.
Heat a 28 cm/11 in frying pan over a medium heat. Add the oil and when it is warm, pour in the eggs and cook for about 5 minutes on one side until almost set.
Slide the *frittata* out of the pan on to a plate, turn over and slide back into the pan, lowering the heat to minimum. Top with the tomatoes and mozzarella, cover with a lid and cook for a further 3 minutes, or until the mozzarella starts to melt. Slide the *frittata* on to a serving platter and top with the rocket (arugula). Serve quite warm.
Serves 6.

FRITTATA DI SEDANO RAPA

Celeriac Frittata

Celeriac is not a very well known vegetable, and I feel sorry about this because I think it is very tasty. I like it not only in soups, which is a common use, but also in salads, stewed or surrounding meat and fish dishes. Fennel is a good substitute.

2 celeriacs, about 600 g/1¹/₄ lb total weight
6 large eggs (U.S. extra large)
120 g/4 oz fontina cheese, grated
2 tbsp extra virgin olive oil
Salt and pepper

Peel the celeriacs and use a grater with large holes to julienne them. Beat the eggs in a large bowl with salt and pepper to taste, then stir in the fontina and celeriac.

Heat half the oil in a non-stick frying pan over a medium heat. Add the celeriac mixture and cook for a few minutes on one side until almost set. Slide out of the pan on to a plate, and turn over. Heat the rest of the oil in the pan. Slide the *frittata* back in to the pan and cook the other side just for 1 minute so it remains almost runny inside. Transfer to a serving platter and serve warm or at room temperature.

Serves 6.

CROSTONI DI UOVA E SPINACI

Toasts with Eggs and Spinach

A very popular antipasto, this is also perfect for a main dish. In fact, I remember being served this for dinner at my parents' table when I was a child.

1 kg/2 lb fresh spinach leaves
120 g/4 oz/1 cup freshly grated parmesan cheese
4 tbsp extra virgin olive oil
6 bread slices
6 large eggs (U.S. extra large)
Salt and pepper

Preheat the oven to 180°C/350°F/Gas 4.
Bring a large pan with a little water to the boil. Add salt and the spinach and cook for about 2 minutes, or until just wilted.
Drain well, squeeze dry and chop finely. Combine with half the parmesan cheese.
Heat half the oil in a large frying pan. Add the spinach and sauté over a medium heat for about 5 minutes. Leave to cool.
Brush the bread slices with the rest of the oil, then arrange on a baking sheet lined with parchment paper. Arrange the spinach on top as a nest. Break an egg into each spinach nest and sprinkle with the rest of the parmesan, and pepper to taste. Cook in the oven for about 10 minutes, or until the egg whites are set. Transfer to a serving platter and serve very warm.

Serves 6.

TIMBALLO DI POLENTA E SALSICCE

Polenta and Sausage Timbal

It is a delicious surprise when you cut the polenta and the juicy sausages fill your dish. You can also replace the sausages with the Meat Sauce on page 178.

240 g/8 oz/2 cups coarse polenta (yellow cornmeal)
1.9 litres/64 fl oz/2 quarts water
1 handful dry porcini mushrooms
2 tbsp extra virgin olive oil
300 g/11 oz sweet Italian. sausages. casings removed
240 ml/8 fl oz/1 cup White Sauce (page 177)
180 g/6 oz mozzarella cheese. diced
Salt and pepper

Bring the water to the boil in a large saucepan. Add salt and the polenta (yellow cornmeal), whisking continuously. Cover the pan, lower the heat to a minimum and cook for 40 minutes.
Meanwhile, cover the mushrooms with water and leave for about 30 minutes.
Preheat the oven to 180°C/350°F/Gas 4.
As soon as the polenta is cooked, wet a 23 cm/9 in mould with cold water and fill with polenta, smoothing the surface with a knife. Press well and let set until cool.
Drain the mushrooms; filter the water and freeze for different preparations. Chop the mushrooms roughly. Heat the oil in a large frying pan over a medium heat.
Add the sausages and crumble with a fork while cooking. After about 5 minutes, combine them in a bowl with the white sauce and the mozzarella cheese.
Add the mushrooms and stir well.
Leaving the polenta in the mould, scoop out about one-third of the inside and fill with the sausage mixture. Cover again with the scooped-out polenta.
Cook in the oven, scooped part up, for about 30 minutes, or until very hot in the centre. Invert on to a warmed serving platter. Serve immediately, while still quite warm.
Serves 6.

TIMBALLO DI TAGLIERINI

Taglierini Timbal

A nice way of presenting a dish of *taglierini*. I like to vary the cheese sometimes using fresh mozzarella or goats' cheese, adding stoned (pitted) olives, anchovies or fried sausages.

300 g/10 oz/2 cups plus 4 tbsp plain (all-purpose) flour
3 large eggs (U.S. extra large)
4 tbsp extra virgin olive oil
480 ml/16 fl oz/2 cups Tomato Sauce (page 178)
180 g/6 oz smoked provola cheese. diced
1 tbsp dried oregano
120 g/4 oz/1 cup freshly grated parmesan cheese
15 g/$^{1}/_{2}$ oz/1 tbsp unsalted butter for buttering the mould
120 g/4 oz/1 cup fine dry breadcrumbs
Salt and pepper

Preheat the oven to 180°C/350°F/Gas 4.
Make the pasta dough with the flour and egg, following the recipe on page 182. Roll out to 0.2 ml/$^{1}/_{8}$ in thick and cut into 0.2 cm/$^{1}/_{8}$ in noodles to make *taglierini*. (Or buy *taglierini*.)
Bring a large pan of water to the boil. Add salt and the *taglierini* and boil until barely *al dente*. Drain well.
Mix with the oil, half the tomato sauce, the provola cheese, oregano, half the parmesan cheese and salt and pepper to taste.
Butter a 2ltr/8 cup ring mould, then coat with the breadcrumbs. Fill with the *taglierini*, pressing them well inside.
Cook in the oven for about 20 minutes, then let rest for about 5 minutes. Invert on to a warmed serving dish, add the rest of the sauce and sprinkle with the remaining Parmesan cheese. Serve quite hot.
Serves 6.

TIMBALLO DI POMODORI E PASTA

Pasta and Tomato Timbal

This well-known Neapolitan recipe was given to me by Jeanne Carola Francesconi, an extraordinary food writer. I never fail to receive many compliments with this recipe, not only for the taste but also for the beauty of the dish.

For the tomatoes:
2 kg/4 lb round, ripe tomatoes
120 g/4 oz/1 cup dry fine breadcrumbs
2 tbsp dry oregano
3 tbsp extra virgin olive oil
2 garlic cloves, finely chopped
For the pasta:
240 g/8 oz zite or rigatoni
480 ml/16 fl oz/2 cups Tomato Sauce (page 178)
240 g/8 oz smoked mozzarella or provola cheese, diced
60 g/2 oz/¹/₂ cup black olives, stoned (pitted) and halved
45 g/1¹/₂ oz/3 tbsp freshly grated parmesan cheese
Oil for greasing the tin
Salt and pepper

Preheat the oven to 180°C/350°F/Gas 4.
Prepare the tomatoes by halving them and discarding the seeds. Sprinkle with salt and let drain in a colander for about 10 minutes. Mix the breadcrumbs with oregano, oil and garlic. Fill the tomato halves with this mixture; reserve 6 tomato halves unfilled. Arrange the filled tomatoes on a baking sheet covered with parchment paper. Bake in the oven for about 30 minutes.
Meanwhile, bring a large saucepan of water to the boil. Add salt and the pasta and cook for about 4 minutes. Drain well, then mix with the cold tomato sauce. Stir in the mozzarella, olives and parmesan cheese.
Grease and line the base and sides of a 23 cm/9 in spring form cake tin, 7.5 cm/3 in deep, with parchment paper. Cover the base with the filled tomatoes, cut side up. Fill with the pasta, press lightly and cover with the unfilled tomatoes, cut side down.
Bake for about 40 minutes. Invert on to a heated serving platter, without lifting off the pan. Leave to rest for about 20 minutes, then lift off the pan and serve immediately.
Serves 6.

PARMIGIANA DI MELANZANE IN FORMA

Moulded Aubergine (Eggplant) Parmigiana

This is a typically elegant Neapolitan preparation. Sometimes I like to use the fried aubergine (eggplant) only to coat the mould and then I fill it with a left-over cooked pasta like penne or fettuccini, mixed with tomato sauce and mozzarella cheese.

6 large long aubergines (eggplants)
960 ml/32 fl oz/4 cups vegetable oil for deep-frying
2 tbsp dry oregano
500 ml/16 fl oz/2 cups Tomato Sauce (page 178)
300 g/10 oz mozzarella cheese, sliced
Salt and pepper

Preheat the oven to 180°C/350°F/Gas 4.
Slice the aubergines (eggplants) lengthwise; do not salt them to drain.
Heat the oil to 180°C/350°F, or until a cube of bread browns in 1 minute in a large frying pan. Fry the aubergines (eggplants), a few at a time, for about 5 minutes until slightly golden. Drain well on paper towels. Sprinkle with the oregano and salt and pepper to taste.
Line a 23 cm/9 in ring mould with aubergine (eggplant) slices and fill with the rest of the aubergines (eggplants), alternating the layers with the tomato sauce and mozzarella; end with a layer of aubergine (eggplant). Cook in the oven for about 20 minutes, or until very hot. Let cool and set for about 5 minutes, then invert on to a warmed serving platter and remove the mould. Serve immediately.
Serves 6.

TIMBALLO DI POLENTA COL CAVOLO NERO

Polenta Timbal with Black Cabbage

Black cabbage is a Tuscan speciality. The leaves are very long, very dark green – almost black – and bubbly. The taste is strong and slightly bitter. If it is not available, use savoy cabbage.

210 g/7 oz/1½ cups dried cannellini beans
600 g/1¼ lb black cabbage
90 g/3 oz pancetta, diced
240 ml/8 fl oz/1 cup chicken stock
240 g/8 oz/2 cups coarse polenta (yellow cornmeal)
1.9 litres/64 fl oz/2 quarts water
Salt and pepper

Cover the beans with water and let stand for about 12 hours. Drain then place in a saucepan, with water to cover. Bring to the boil, lower the heat, cover and cook for about 1½ hour, or until soft. Drain. Meanwhile, finely shred the cabbage, discarding the tough cores.
Fry the *pancetta* in a large frying pan over a medium heat for about 10 minutes until barely golden, stirring with a wooden spoon occasionally. Stir in the cabbage and let it cook for a few minutes then pour in the stock. Cover the pan, lower the heat and cook for about 40 minutes. Uncover, add the beans and let the excess liquid evaporate. Add salt and pepper to taste. Meanwhile, bring the water to the boil. Add salt to taste and the polenta (yellow cornmeal), whisking continuously. Cover the pan, lower the heat to a minimum and cook for 40 minutes.
As soon as the polenta is cooked, wet a 2 lb mould with cold water and fill with polenta, smoothing the surface with a knife. Press well and let rest a few minutes to set then invert on to a warmed serving platter and remove the mould. Surround with the cabbage and cannellini beans. Serve immediately, while still very hot.
Serves 6

Opposite page: Pasta and Tomato Timbal

TIMBALLO DI FAGIOLINI

Green Bean Timbal

This style of *timbal*, or flan as we used to call it, is very popular in Italy. The procedure is always the same, but you can vary the vegetables, including carrots, broccoli, courgettes (zucchini), spinach or Swiss chard. And if you want to turn it into a richer and more substantial dish, serve with a Meat Sauce or Tomato Sauce (like the ones on page 178) or sautéed veal scaloppine or sweetbreads.

15 g/^{1}/$_2$ oz/1 tbsp unsalted butter
60 g/2 oz/^{1}/$_2$ cup finely grated dry breadcrumbs
500 g/1 lb green beans
3 tbsp extra virgin olive oil
240 ml/8 fl oz/1 cup White Sauce (page 177)
60 g/2 oz freshly grated parmesan cheese
3 large eggs (U.S. extra large)
Salt and pepper

Preheat the oven to 180°C/350°F/Gas 4. Butter a 25 cm/10 in ring mould then coat with the breadcrumbs. Set aside.
Bring a large pan of water to the boil. Add salt and the beans and cook for about 10 minutes or until tender; the exact cooking time depends on how fresh they are. Drain well.
Heat the oil in a large frying pan over a medium heat. Add the beans and sauté for a couple of minutes. Sprinkle with pepper to taste and stir in the white sauce.
Transfer the beans to a blender. Add the parmesan cheese and the eggs and blend a couple of minutes until creamy. Spoon into the prepared ring mould and smooth the surface with a knife. Place in a roasting pan with enough water to come half way up the side of the mould. Bake in the oven for about 50 minutes. Let it cool slightly, then invert on to a warmed serving platter and remove the mould. Fill the centre with your preferred sauce and spoon some around the side. Serve very warm.
Serves 6.

SFORMATO DI BROCCOLI

Broccoli Mould

The broccoli can be replaced with spinach, Swiss chard, peas, carrots or green beans, everything blanched or boiled before sautéeing.

15 g/^{1}/$_2$ oz/1 tbsp unsalted butter for buttering the mould
60 g/2 oz/^{1}/$_2$ cup dry fine breadcrumbs
500 g/1 lb broccoli stems and florets
300 g/10 oz/2 cups boiling potatoes, peeled and julienned
3 tbsp extra virgin olive oil
60 g/2 oz/^{1}/$_2$ cup freshly grated parmesan cheese
3 large eggs, beaten (U.S. extra large)
Salt and pepper

Preheat the oven to 180°C/350°F/Gas 4. Butter a 25 cm/10 in ring mould, then coat with the breadcrumbs; set aside. Peel the broccoli stems, then slice them thinly. Bring a large pan of water to the boil. Add salt, the broccoli stems and the potatoes and when the water comes to the boil again add the broccoli florets. Boil for about 3 minutes. Drain. Heat the oil in a large frying pan over a low heat. Add the broccoli and potato mixture and cook until all the moisture evaporates. Pass everything through a food mill or food processor. Stir in the parmesan cheese, the eggs and pepper to taste, stirring until well blended.
Fill the ring mould with the broccoli mixture. Place in a roasting pan with enough hot water to come half way up the side of the mould. Bake in the oven for about 1 hour. Invert on to a warmed serving platter and remove the mould. Serve immediately, while still quite hot.
Serves 6.

SFORMATO DI PATATE E SPINACI

Spinach and Potato Mould

I often serve this mould at Coltibuono when my in-laws visit. I surround it with an egg sauce and serve it as a *Piatto de Mezzo* after the soup and before the meat dish. The children keep quiet throughout the meal.

60 g/2 oz/¼ cup unsalted butter
120 g/4 oz/1 cup freshly grated parmesan cheese
1 kg/2 lb unpeeled boiling potatoes
1 kg/2 lb fresh spinach leaves
3 large eggs (U.S. extra large)
Salt and pepper

Preheat the oven to 180°C/350°F/Gas 4. Use half the butter to butter a 27.5 cm/11 in ring mould and coat with half the cheese; set aside. Bring a large pan of water to the boil. Add salt and the potatoes and boil for about 30 minutes, until very soft. When cool enough to handle, peel and mash while still warm. Meanwhile, blanch the spinach in little boiling water for about 3 minutes until just wilted. Drain, squeeze well and chop finely. Add to the potatoes and leave to cool. Stir in the eggs, the rest of the butter, the rest of the cheese and salt and pepper to taste.
Fill the prepared mould with the potato and spinach mixture, smoothing the surface with a knife. Bake in the oven for about 50 minutes, or until the mixture shrinks and moves from the sides slightly. If it browns too much on the top, cover with aluminium foil. Invert on to a warmed serving platter and remove the mould. Serve immediately, while still quite hot.
Serves 6.

SUFFLÉ DI POLENTA E RADICCHIO

Polenta and Radicchio Soufflé

Polenta can be coarse cornmeal or a finer yellow or even white. The coarse yellow variety is used mostly in Lombardy and Piedmont, while the fine white or yellow is favoured in Venezia. Look for polenta flour in health food shops if not in the nearest supermarket.

1 litre/1¾ pints/4½ cups milk
240 g/8 oz/2 cups coarse polenta (yellow cornmeal)
300 g/10 oz red radicchio
60 g/2 oz bacon
60 g/2 oz/4 tbsp unsalted butter, plus 15 g/½ oz/1 tbsp for buttering the soufflé dish
120 g/4 oz/1 cup freshly grated parmesan cheese
3 large eggs (U.S. extra large)
Salt and pepper

Bring the milk to the boil in a large saucepan. Add salt and the polenta in a steady stream, whisking constantly. Continue stirring with a wooden spoon and cook for about 40 minutes. Remove from the heat and leave to cool.
Meanwhile, julienne the radicchio and chop the bacon.
Preheat the oven to 200°C/400°F/Gas 4. Butter a 25 cm/10 in soufflé dish with half the butter, then coat with half the parmesan cheese; set aside.
Fry the bacon in a frying pan over a medium heat until golden, stirring occasionally. Add the radicchio, lower the heat and cook for about 5 minutes, or until tender; leave to cool.
Add the egg yolks, the rest of the parmesan cheese and the rest of the butter to the polenta, stirring until well blended. Stir in the radicchio and bacon. Beat the egg whites until stiff, then fold them into the polenta very delicately.
Spoon the polenta mixture into the soufflé dish. Bake in the oven for about 40 minutes, or until well puffed and golden on top. Serve immediately.
Serves 6.

COLD FORK FOOD,
INSALATE, CARPACCI, TERRINE

INSALATE ARE SALADS AND TRADITIONALLY ITALIANS LIKE THEIRS AS SIMPLE AS POSSIBLE: FRESH GREENS DRESSED WITH EXTRA VIRGIN OLIVE OIL AND RED WINE VINEGAR. MORE AND MORE, HOWEVER, COMBINATION SALADS, MADE WITH A VARIETY OF INGREDIENTS AND SOMETIMES EVEN WITHOUT GREENS, ARE BECOMING POPULAR AS ANTIPASTI. THE MIXTURE USUALLY FEATURES CLASSIC COMBINATIONS OF FOODS AND TASTES, FOR INSTANCE, BEANS AND PORK, RAW MUSHROOMS AND PARMESAN CHEESE, PRESENTED ON A BED OF LETTUCE.

I have also included some more creative combinations that I find work well, for example, smoked trout with figs, and chick-peas with caviar. In these two recipes the figs and chick-peas give the dish a classic Italian flavour, while the smoked trout and caviar add a more unusual taste. You will find many versions of the delicious contemporary dish called *carpaccio*. The original recipe was invented in 1950 by Giuseppe Cipriani, founder of *Harry's Bar* in Venezia. He named it after the celebrated Venetian Renaissance painter, Vittore Carpaccio, who was known for his unusual use of brilliant reds and white, the attractive colours of this dish. It consists of very finely sliced raw beef sirloin dressed with a mayonnaise made with a pinch of powdered mustard and Worchestershire sauce, drizzled *"alla Kandisky"*, as Arrigo Cipriani, son of Giuseppe, describes the desired decorative effect.

Another similar contemporary dish from Piemonte is called *carne all'albese*. The base of this dish is also raw beef but dressed

with shavings of parmesan cheese, topped with flakes of white truffles or *porcini* mushrooms, and seasoned with olive oil and lemon. I have created several other *carpaccio* combinations. Fish prepared in this way is especially successful. It may come as a surprise to learn that *terrine* is an Italian dish, literally, as well as in a culinary sense. *Terrine* are little terracotta pots used to hold the ingredients of a *terrine*. The French not only adopted the Italian dish but also the Italian name, as did the English. The French word would be *tureen*.

Terrine were popular in Renaissance times, when they were probably exported to France. My mother was fond of them and I made my first *terrine* when I was a very little girl. They are not difficult and it might come as a relief to know you do not have to go to a French deli to buy an Italian terrine.

Italians use less butter and fat than the French in their terrine, and make them more meaty. Game is a popular ingredient, and contemporary chefs are now making fish terrines.

La legatura del cespo rende più bianche e più tenere, e quindi maggiormente apprezzate, le foglie della lattuga romana

INSALATA DI CAVOLO CAPPUCCIO E SPECK

Cabbage and Speck Salad

A speciality from Friuli, a region famous for its wines, *speck* is a smoked ham, now sold around the world. It's very versatile, and I often substitute it for the more traditional *pancetta*, which often seems too fatty for modern dishes.

300 g/10 oz white cabbage
2 apples, such as Granny Smith
3 tbsp plain yogurt
3 tbsp milk
1 tsp lemon juice
1 tsp mustard
15 g/¹/₂ oz/1 tbsp unsalted butter
300 g/10 oz speck, sliced paper thin
Salt

Finely shred the cabbage and arrange on a serving platter. Peel and thinly slice the apples, then arrange on the cabbage. Stir together the yogurt, milk, lemon juice, mustard and salt to taste, and sprinkle on the salad. Toss carefully.
Melt the butter in a frying pan over a medium heat. Add the *speck* and heat through for a couple of minutes, turning once. Drain. Arrange on the salad and serve immediately.
Serve 6.

INSALATA DI TACCHINO ALL' UVA

Turkey Salad with Grapes

A very useful dish after Thanksgiving or Christmas when you have to contend with leftover turkey. This is also delicious with roasted chicken or veal.

1 head escarole
1 head curly endive (chicory)
210 g/7 oz black grapes
210 g/7 oz white grapes
2 small Bosch pears
500 g/1 lb/3 cups boneless leftover roast turkey, skinned and diced
6 walnuts, shelled and chopped
2 tbsp balsamic vinegar
4 tbsp extra virgin olive oil
1 pinch grated fresh horseradish
Salt

Tear the escarole and endive (chicory) into small pieces and arrange on a serving platter. Peel and halve the black and white grapes and seed (pit) them. Arrange on the salad. Peel and dice the pears and arrange on top, along with the turkey and walnuts. Combine the vinegar, olive oil, horseradish and salt to taste. Pour over the salad and toss delicately. Serve at room temperature.
Serves 6.

INSALATA DI MELE E FINOCCHIO AI CAPPERI

Apple and Fennel Salad with Caper Sauce

Most Italians like their salads with only extra virgin olive oil and red wine vinegar, but occasionally I add a few different ingredients for variety and interest.

150 g/5 oz white cabbage
90 g/3 oz red radicchio
2 apples such as Granny Smith
1 handful rocket (arugula)
2 fennel bulbs
1 tbsp capers in vinegar, drained
1 tbsp red wine vinegar
1/2 tsp mustard powder
1 large egg yolk (U.S. extra large)
1 handful chopped fresh flat-leaf parsley
6 tbsp extra virgin olive oil
Salt and pepper

Finely shred the cabbage and radicchio. Slice and peel the apples, but do not peel. Tear the rocket (arugula) into small pieces. Discard the outer leaves of the fennel, thinly slice the remainder.
Arrange all the ingredients in a salad bowl. Put the capers, vinegar, mustard, egg yolk, parsley, oil and salt and pepper to taste in a blender or food processor and blend until creamy. Pour on the salad and toss.
Serve immediately.
Serves 6.

INSALATA DI CECI E CAVIALE ROSSO

Chick-pea and Red Caviar Salad

Chick-peas take a long time to cook, but you can cook them one day ahead and keep in the refrigerator. Just let them come back to room temperature before serving. Salted herring and trout are good alternatives for the red caviar.

300 g/10 oz/2 cups dried chick-peas
1 small sweet onion
1 head Boston lettuce
Grated zest of 1 lemon
1 tbsp red wine vinegar
4 tbsp extra virgin olive oil
2 hard-cooked eggs
120 g/4 oz/1/2 cup red caviar
Salt and pepper

Cover the chick-peas with water and let stand for about 12 hours. Drain, then place in a saucepan, with water to cover. Bring to the boil, then lower the heat and cook for about 2 1/2 hours, or until tender. Drain, put into a large bowl and leave to cool completely. Slice the onion thinly and tear the lettuce into small pieces. Add to the bowl with the lemon zest, vinegar, oil and salt and pepper to taste. Toss well, then arrange on a serving platter.
Shell the eggs and separate the white from the yolks. Pass them both through a fine sieve on top of the salad. Top with the red caviar. Serve immediately.
Serves 6.

INSALATA DI FICHI E TROTA AFFUMICATA

Smoked Trout and Fig Salad

Francesco, the wonderful and creative chef at *Osteria di Rendola* near Montevarchi – one of the best restaurants in Tuscany – serves this salad in autumn.

300 g/10 oz mixed salad greens, such as mâche, rocket (arugula) and lettuce
210 g/7 oz smoked trout fillets
1 tbsp balsamic vinegar
4 tbsp extra virgin olive oil
6 figs
30 g/1 oz/¼ cup pine nuts
Salt and pepper

Tear the salad greens into small pieces and arrange on a serving platter. Slice the trout fillets and arrange them on the salad.
Combine the vinegar with the oil and salt to taste in a bowl, then sprinkle on the salad. Toss thoroughly. Peel the figs and quarter them. Arrange on the salad and sprinkle with the pine nuts.
Serve at room temperature.
Serves 6.

INSALATA AUTUNNALE

Porcini and Grape Salad

Autumn is the time to enjoy this because fresh *porcini* are available everywhere and grapes are very tasty. At other times, substitute button mushrooms for the *porcini*, although they are not so tasty.

300 g/10 oz wild porcini mushrooms
1 ripe avocado
300 g/10 oz white grapes
1 handful rocket (arugula)
120 g/4 oz/½ cup plain yogurt
2 tbsp extra virgin olive oil
1 tsp sweet paprika
Salt

Wipe the porcini, but do not rinse, then slice thinly. Peel and slice the avocado. Peel, halve and seed the grapes.
Arrange the rocket (arugula) on a serving platter. Top with *porcini*, avocado and grapes. Mix the yogurt with the oil and a little salt. Pour over the salad and sprinkle with paprika. Serve immediately.
Serves 6.

INSALATA DI LATTUGA AL CAVIALE

Lettuce Leaves with Red Caviar

A very crispy lettuce like iceberg is perfect for this salad. If you really feel generous, you can add a couple of spoons of beluga or sevruga caviar for a richer taste.

210 g/7oz iceberg lettuce
1 ripe avocado
150 g/5 oz red caviar or lump fish roe
6 tbsp soured (sour) cream
1 tsp paprika
Salt

Rinse the lettuce, carefully dry and arrange the leaves on a serving platter. Peel and slice the avocado and arrange on top of the lettuce. Sprinkle with the caviar, soured (sour) cream, salt to taste and a little paprika.
Serve at room temperature.
Serves 6.

Opposite page: Smoked Trout and Fig Salad

INSALATA DI POLLO ALL' UVETTA

Chicken Salad with Raisins

This salad can be served warm or at room temperature. If the chicken is warm, make sure you serve it immediately so that it doesn't wilt the bed of lettuce. It is a speciality of my friend Pinky Banfield, who kindly invites a few friends to her beautiful house after *La Scala* opera performances. It is ideal for this occasion when everything has to be ready for the guests' arrival.

150 g/5 oz/²/₃ cup ricotta cheese
3 tbsp raisins, soaked in water for about 30 minutes
and drained
3 tbsp pine nuts
2 large egg yolks (U.S. extra large)
2 chicken breast halves not separated (1 whole chicken breast),
butterflied
15 g/¹/₂ oz/1 tbsp unsalted butter
3 tbsp extra virgin olive oil
1 tbsp red wine vinegar
300 g/10 oz Boston lettuce
Salt and pepper

Combine the ricotta cheese, raisins, pine nuts, egg yolks and salt and pepper to taste in a bowl. Spread the mixture on top of the butterflied chicken, then roll up. Tie tightly with a kitchen string.
Melt the butter and 1 tbsp of the oil in a large frying pan over a medium heat. Add the chicken roll and cook until slightly golden, turning it a few times. This should take about 10 minutes. Add a little water to keep moist, cover with a lid and cook for about 20 minutes. Remove the roll from the cooking juices and leave to cool.
Tear the salad into small pieces and arrange on a serving platter. Combine the rest of the oil with the vinegar and salt to taste, then pour over the salad. Untie the meat and slice thinly. Arrange the slices on top of the lettuce and serve.
Serves 6.

INSALATA DI FAGIOLI E PANCETTA

Bean Salad with Pancetta

The beans I prefer to use in this are *borlotti*, a typical Italian bean with red spots, but *cannellini* beans work just as well. The *pancetta* can also be replaced with smoked bacon that will add an extra flavour.

300 g/10 oz/2 cups dried borlotti beans
210 g/7 oz pancetta, diced
1 large onion, thinly sliced
1 sprig rosemary
4 tbsp red wine vinegar
3 tbsp extra virgin olive oil
Salt and pepper

Place the beans in a saucepan, cover with cold water and bring slowly to the boil. Lower the heat and cook for about 2 hours until tender. Drain and keep warm. Cook the *pancetta* in a frying pan with the onion over a medium heat for about 10 minutes, or until crispy and golden, stirring frequently. Add the rosemary, then pour off the fat and stir in the vinegar. Cook a couple of minutes until all the liquid evaporates. Check the salt.
Arrange the beans and the *pancetta* on a platter and sprinkle with pepper to taste. Drizzle with the olive oil. Serve warm, lukewarm or at room temperature.
Serves 6.

INSALATA DI GAMBERI E ASPARAGI

Prawn (Shrimp) and Asparagus Salad

The best salad leaf for this is mâche but, if it is not available, Webb or Boston lettuce is a good substitute. This recipe is from one of the best fish restaurants in Italy, Antonio in Castlenuovo Berardenga. He serves the catch of the day steamed with olive oil and vegetables, prepared with incredible love. I like to go to the restaurant at least once a month.

300 g/10 oz asparagus tips
300 g/10 oz uncooked prawns (shrimp), deveined
210 g/7 oz mâche
1 tsp lemon juice
3 tbsp extra virgin olive oil
Grated zest of 1 lemon
Salt and pepper

Separately bring 2 pans of water to the boil. Add the asparagus tips to one pan and the prawns (shrimp) to the other and cook for only a couple of minutes.
Drain and cool to room temperature.
Rinse the mâche and arrange on a serving platter. Top with the warm asparagus and prawns, then sprinkle with salt and pepper to taste, lemon juice, oil and finally the lemon zest and serve.
Serves 6.

INSALATA AL COCCO

Grated Coconut Salad

A very refreshing and unusual salad that is easy to make because grated coconut can be bought in most supermarkets. In season you can substitute grated courgettes (zucchini) and carrots, or fennel bulbs, white celery or yellow or red (bell) peppers.

2 courgettes (zucchini)
2 carrots
300 g/10 oz white cabbage or savoy cabbage
1 garlic clove
1 handful rocket (arugula)
6 red radishes
1 tbsp red wine vinegar
4 tbsp extra virgin olive oil
3 tbsp grated unsweetened coconut
Salt

Clean and finely shred the courgettes (zucchini), carrots and cabbage. Chop the garlic. Tear the rocket (arugula) into small pieces. Slice the radishes. Arrange all the ingredients in a salad bowl. Dissolve salt to taste with the vinegar, then pour on top of the vegetables. Add the oil and toss together. Sprinkle with the coconut and serve.
Serves 6.

INSALATA DI CARPACCIO

Carpaccio Salad

This typical Piedmontese meat salad has several variations. The egg yolk gives a nice creamy texture, but it can be omitted. Vegetables in vinegar or oil are readily available in supermarkets and from Italian delicatessens, but you can prepare them at home, following the recipes in Part IV.

60 g/1¼ lb lean beef, such as top round or eye round
2 garlic cloves
60 g/2 oz cucumbers in vinegar, drained
60 g/12 oz/4 tbsp capers in vinegar or oil, drained
3 anchovy fillets in oil, drained
1 handful fresh flat-leaf parsley
1 celery stalk
Juice of 2 lemons
3 egg yolks
4 tbsp extra virgin olive oil
300 g/10 oz rocket (arugula)
Salt and pepper

Using a sharp knife, chop the meat finely. Chop the garlic, cucumbers, capers, anchovies, parsley and celery.
Combine the meat with the chopped vegetables in a bowl. Add the lemon juice, egg yolks, olive oil and salt and pepper to taste, and stir to blend the flavours.
Form 6 patties with the meat.
Cover a serving platter with the rocket (arugula) and arrange the patties on top. Serve immediately.
Serves 6.

CARPACCIO DI PESCE AL RAFANO

Fish Carpaccio with Horseradish

This dressing is also excellent on boiled potatoes, courgettes (zucchini) or carrots, grilled red radicchio, or poached fish, such as salmon or cod.

1 large egg plus 1 extra yolk (U.S. extra large)
120 ml/4 fl oz/½ cup extra virgin olive oil
1 tbsp grated fresh horseradish
1 anchovy fillet in oil, drained
Juice of ½ lemon
1 garlic clove
600 g/1¼ lb firm fish, such as tuna, salmon or swordfish
Salt and pepper

Put the egg and extra yolk in a blender and blend. With the motor still running, add the oil in a steady stream until a mayonnaise forms. Add the horseradish, anchovy, lemon juice and the garlic and blend again until creamy. Add salt and pepper to taste and transfer to a serving bowl.
Slice the fish paper thin and arrange on a serving platter. Serve with the horseradish sauce.
Serves 6.

CARPACCIO AL FINOCCHIO E FAVE

*Meat Carpaccio with Fennel
and Broad (Fava) Beans*

To slice meat really paper thin, put it in the freezer for about one hour before slicing. Use top round or eye round beef.

500 g/1 lb lean beef
2 fennel bulbs
1 kg/2 lb very fresh broad (fava) beans
Juice and grated zest of 1 lemon
6 tbsp extra virgin olive oil
Salt and pepper

Slice the meat paper thin and arrange slightly curled on a serving platter.
Discard the tough outer leaves of the fennel and slice paper thin vertically. Peel the broad (fava) beans, and if they are bitter remove the thin inner skin as well – in this case, buy double quantity.
Arrange the fennel on top of the meat and the broad (fava) beans around. Sprinkle with the lemon juice and zest and salt and pepper to taste. Pour over the olive oil. Serve at room temperature.
Serves 6.

CARPACCIO DI PESCE AI FINOCCHIO E BALSAMICO

*Fish Carpaccio with Fennel
and Balsamic Vinegar*

I use monkfish for this recipe because it is delicate and tasty, but fillets of sole or salmon will also do.

500 g/1 lb very fresh monkfish
150 g/5 oz mixed green salad leaves as mâche and Cos lettuce
3 tbsp balsamic vinegar
3 tbsp extra virgin olive oil
1 fennel bulb
Salt and pepper

Slice the fish paper thin. Tear the salad leaves into small pieces and arrange on a serving platter.
Arrange the fish on top and sprinkle with the balsamic vinegar, olive oil and salt and pepper to taste.
Clean the fennel, discarding the outer tough leaves, then halve and slice the bulb paper thin; reserve the green fronds. Sprinkle the fish with the fennel and garnish with the fronds. Serve at room temperature.
Serves 6.

PECORINO AL PEPE E OLIO

Marinated Pecorino Cheese with Oil and Pepper

A very popular recipe in Coltibuono's restaurant especially in the springtime when pecorino is still fresh and the oil has been pressed only three months before and still has the pungent taste. This is a 'must' as an accompaniment to fresh broad (fava) beans.

300 g/10 oz fresh Tuscan or Sardinian pecorino cheese, rind removed
6 tbsp extra virgin olive oil
Pepper

Cut the cheese into bite-size pieces, then arrange on a serving platter and sprinkle with the oil and pepper. Leave for about 1 hour before serving with cocktail sticks (toothpicks).
Serves 6.

PECORINO AL FINOCCHIO

Pecorino Cheese with Wild Fennel

For this buy a medium fresh pecorino cheese. Tuscan quality is the nicest, but Sardinian is also good, although a little stronger and saltier. Avoid the Romano versions, as they are usually of a cheap quality.

6 slices pecorino cheese, rind removed
2 tbsp fennel seeds
6 wild fennel flowers or some green leaves from fennel bulbs
6 tbsp extra virgin olive oil
Pepper

Arrange the pecorino slices on individual dishes. Put the seeds in a spice grinder or coffee mill and blend until powdered, then sprinkle over the cheese. Garnish with the fennel flowers, pour the oil on top, and sprinkle with pepper to taste. Serve.
Serves 6.

MOSCARDINI AL SEDANO

Baby Octopus with Celeriac

Baby octopus should be really small like the ones served at my favourite Roman restaurant, *Rosetta*, at the Pantheon. They should be only about 2.5 cm/1 in long, or they will be tough. If you cannot find them, substitute prawns (shrimp).

600 g/1¼ lb baby octopus
1 small onion
1 carrot
1 celery stalk
2 hard-cooked eggs
1 celeriac
Juice of ½ lemon
1 pomegranate
4 tbsp extra virgin olive oil
2 tbsp snipped fresh chives or flat-leaf parsley
Salt and pepper

Wash the octopus. Bring a large pan of water to the boil. Add the onion, carrot and celery and simmer for about 30 minutes. Discard the vegetables, then add the octopus and simmer for only a couple of minutes until very tender. Drain and leave to cool to room temperature.
Shred and chop the whites and the yolks of the eggs separately. Peel the celeriac and finely shred. Sprinkle with the lemon juice. Peel the pomegranates and reserve the seeds.
Combine the octopus with the celeriac, shredded egg and pomegranate seeds and arrange on a platter. Sprinkle with salt and pepper to taste the pomegranate seeds. Drizzle with the oil. Toss delicately. Sprinkle with the chives and serve immediately.
Serves 6.

Opposite page: Marinated Pecorino Cheese with Oil and Pepper

TERRINA DI FEGATINI E PANE

Chicken Liver and Bread Terrine

A very traditional Tuscan dish I like to serve with a glass of *vin santo*, the Tuscan dessert wine that is also like the French Sauternes.

300 g/10 oz coarse country bread, crusts removed
500 ml/14 fl oz/2 cups milk
45 g/1¹/₂ oz/3 tbsp unsalted butter
6 large bay leaves, preferably fresh
500 g/1 lb chicken livers, thawed if frozen, and trimmed
3 eggs
60 ml/2 fl oz/¹/₄ cup vin santo
Salt and pepper

Put the bread in a bowl, pour over the milk and leave it to absorb for about 30 minutes, stirring it a couple of times.
Preheat the oven to 180°C/350°F/Gas 4. Butter a rectangular 23 cm/9 in mould with 15 g/¹/₂ oz/1 tbsp of the butter. Cover the bottom with the bay leaves; set aside.
Melt the rest of the butter in a frying pan over a medium heat. Add the chicken livers and sauté for about 5 minutes, stirring occasionally. Sprinkle with salt and pepper to taste. Transfer to a blender and blend until creamy. Squeeze the bread from the milk and place in a bowl. Add the chicken livers, eggs and *vin santo* and stir until well blended.
Fill mould with the liver mixture. Cover with foil and place a 23 cm/10 in in a roasting pan with enough water to come half way up the side of the mould. Cook in the oven for 1 hour until all liquid has evaporated. Let cool slightly, then invert on to a serving platter and remove the mould. Leave to cool at room temperature before serving.
Serves 6.

TERRINA DI GAMBERI AL DRAGONCELLO

Prawn (Shrimp) Terrine with Tarragon

Fresh tarragon can be difficult to find, especially in winter. I suggest you buy a large quantity when you can and keep it already chopped in a plastic bag in the freezer. It is very tasty on fish, with peas or courgettes (zucchini) and sautéed veal scaloppine.

600 g/1¹/₄ lb uncooked prawns (shrimp), peeled and deveined
210 g/7 oz/³/₄ cup plus 2 tbsp ricotta cheese
4 tbsp extra virgin olive oil
2 tbsp lemon juice
3 tbsp finely chopped fresh tarragon
Salt and pepper

Bring a large pan of water to the boil. Add the prawns (shrimp) and cook for about 2 minutes until they turn pink, depending how big the prawn (shrimp) tails are. Drain and leave to cool. Place the prawns (shrimp) in a food processor, with the ricotta cheese, 3 tbsp of the oil, the lemon juice, tarragon and salt and pepper to taste, and blend until creamy.
Use the rest of the oil to brush a rectangular 23 cm/10 in mould. Fill with the fish mixture and leave to cool. When it is cooled place in the refrigerator for 24 hours. To unmould, run a round-bladed knife all around, then insert on to a platter and remove the mould. Serve at room temperature.
Serves 6.

PÂTÉ DI CONIGLIO

Rabbit Pâté

With food processors it is very easy to prepare home-made pâté – it's just a question of a good balance of the meats and herbs or other flavourings and not too much butter to keep the texture light.

210 g/7 oz flat pancetta, sliced paper thin
300 g/10 oz boneless rabbit
300 g/10 oz lean boneless pork
180 g/6 oz/³/₄ cup ricotta cheese
1 large egg (U.S. extra large)
1 tbsp juniper berries
60 g/2 oz/4 tbsp unsalted butter
Salt and pepper

Preheat the oven to 180°C/350°F/Gas 4. Line a 25 cm/10 in long pâté terrine with slightly overlapping *pancetta* slices. Put the rabbit, pork, ricotta, egg, juniper berries, butter and salt and pepper to taste into a food processor fitted with a metal blade. Process until well blended. Fill the mould with the rabbit mixture and cover with more overlapping *pancetta* slices. Cover and seal with aluminium foil.

Place in a roasting pan with enough hot water to come half way up the sides of the terrine. Bake in the oven for about 1¹/₂ hours, or until the liquid on top of the meat is completely transparent. While the pâté is cooling put a weight of about 240 g/8 oz on top, this will make it easier to slice. It will take about 2 hours to cool. When cool, invert on to a platter and remove the mould. Slice and serve.
Serves 6.

POMODORI RIPIENI AI GAMBERI E FAGIOLI

Tomatoes Filled with Prawns (Shrimp) and Beans

I always like to dilute pesto sauce with a little water to make it more delicate, and I suggest you never to buy commercial pesto, because it takes only two minutes to make in a blender.

6 large tomatoes
90 g/3 oz dried beans, such as cannellini or Great Northerns
120 ml/4 fl oz/¹/₂ cup extra virgin olive oil, plus 2 tbsp
210 g/7 oz uncooked prawns (shrimp)
2 handfuls basil leaves
2 garlic cloves
2 tbsp pine nuts
2 tbsp freshly grated pecorino cheese
2 tbsp freshly grated parmesan cheese
Salt and pepper

Cut off the upper part of the tomatoes, then scoop out the seeds and tough parts. Sprinkle with salt, place in a colander and leave them to drain upside down for a couple of hours. Meanwhile, bring the beans to the boil, cover and allow to cook for about 1¹/₂ hours over a low heat until tender. Drain and leave to cool.

Heat 2 tbsp of the oil in a frying pan over a medium heat. Add the prawns (shrimp) and sauté for about 2 minutes until pink. Remove from the heat and leave to cool.

Put the rest of the oil, the basil, garlic, pine nuts and pecorino and Parmesan cheese, into a blender. Add a little salt and pepper to taste and blend until creamed. Add 120 ml/4 fl oz/¹/₂ cup water and blend for a further few seconds.

Combine the beans, prawns and pesto sauce, then use to fill the tomatoes. Arrange on a platter and serve.
Serves 6.

ARANCE AI DATTERI E CIPOLLE

Oranges with Dates and Onions

A Sicilian speciality that I particularly cherish combining sweet-and-sour flavours. You can make many variations on this recipe, such as replacing the dates with pomegranate seeds or black olives.

6 oranges
18 dates
2 white onions
4 tbsp extra virgin olive oil

Peel the oranges and slice them crosswise, peeling away the bitter white pith, or cut into wedges with a sharp knife. Stone (pit) the dates. Peel the onions and slice them paper thin.
Arrange the oranges and dates on a serving platter, and cover with the onions. Pour over the oil and serve immediately at room temperature.
Serves 6.

RUCOLA IN INSALATA CON PERE E PARMIGIANO

Pears, Parmesan and Rocket (Arugula) Salad

Salads should usually be prepared at the last minute, especially if they are composed of raw ingredients, like this one. In any case, never keep a salad in the refrigerator, and never serve it cold. Always at room temperature.

210 g/7 oz rocket (arugula)
3 Bosch pears, not too ripe
Juice of 1 lemon
210 g/7 oz parmesan cheese
4 tbsp extra virgin olive oil
Salt and pepper

Wash the rocket (arugula). Dry and tear into small pieces. Arrange in a salad bowl. Peel the pears and slice thinly. Sprinkle with the lemon juice and arrange on the salad. Slice the parmesan cheese paper thin and arrange half on top of the pears. Sprinkle with salt and pepper to taste. Add the oil and toss delicately. Place the rest of the Parmesan on top.
Serve immediately.
Serves 6.

MELE ALLA CREMA DI GORGONZOLA

Apples with Gorgonzola Cream

The tartness of the apples perfectly matches the pungent taste of the gorgonzola cheese. Remember that fresh gorgonzola is quite white and not too smelly.

6 apples, such as Granny Smith
Juice of 1 lemon
120 ml/4 fl oz/1½ cup double (heavy) cream
210 g/7 oz very fresh gorgonzola cheese
6 walnuts, shelled and chopped

Peel, core and slice the apples, then arrange them on a serving platter. Sprinkle with the lemon juice so they do not brown. Put the cream and Gorgonzola cheese in a pan over a low heat and heat until it melts, stirring with a wooden spoon. Leave to cool, then pour on top of the apples. Sprinkle with the walnuts.
Serve immediately.
Serves 6.

Opposite page: Oranges with Dates and Onions

INSALATA DI FINOCCHIO AGLI AGRUMI

Fennel Salad with Oranges and Grapefruit

If you do not like the combination of the sweetness of the fennels with the acidity of orange and grapefruit, replace the citrus fruit with thinly sliced parmesan cheese or shredded fontina cheese.

6 fennel bulbs
1 orange
1 grapefruit
4 tbsp extra virgin olive oil
Salt and pepper

Remove the outer leaves of the fennel bulbs. Cut the bulbs in half, rinse well and vertically slice them thinly. Arrange on a serving platter. Peel the orange and grapefruit, and cut into wedges, discarding the bitter white pith. Sprinkle the fennel with salt and pepper to taste, pour over the oil and mix carefully. Add the orange and grapefruit wedges. Serve immediately.
Serves 6.

INSALATA DI ARANCE E POMPELMI ALLA MAIONESE

Orange and Grapefruit Salad with Mayonnaise

This salad looks very nice if the fruit is diced and arranged in the emptied half grapefruit shells. Another attractive presentation is also the traditional one, which I describe below.

3 oranges, preferably blood
3 grapefruit
240 ml/8 fl oz/1 cup Mayonnaise (page 177), or good-quality commercial
4 tbsp milk
6 black (ripe) olives, halves and stoned (pitted)
3 spring onions (scallions), thinly sliced
1 handful fresh mint leaves

Peel the oranges and grapefruits, cutting away the bitter white pith. Cut both into slices and arrange overlapping and alternated on a serving platter. Blend the mayonnaise with the milk and pour on top of the fruits. Garnish with the olives and onions. Sprinkle with the mint and serve at room temperature.
Serves 6.

TARTARA ALLA RUCOLA

Chopped Steak Tartare with Rocket (Arugula)

Chop the meat with a knife – it is a little more difficult than doing it in a food processor but it makes such a difference to the taste.

600 g/20 oz top or eye round of beef
300 g/10 oz rocket (arugula)
Juice of 2 lemons
6 anchovy fillets in oil, drained and chopped
1 tbsp Worchestershire sauce
3 tbsp whole green peppercorns
3 tbsp extra virgin olive oil
6 large egg yolks (U.S. extra large)
Salt

Finely chop the beef and rocket (arugula) separately. Put the beef in a bowl with one-third of the rocket (arugula), the lemon juice, anchovies, Worchestershire sauce, green peppercorns, olive oil and salt to taste. Stir until well blended.
Form into 6 equal-size balls and press them in the centre to make 6 cavities. Arrange the meat on individual dishes, surround with the rest of the rocket and top the cavities with the egg yolks. Serve immediately.
Serves 6.

Opposite page: Fennel Salad with Oranges and Grapefruit

FICHI CON FORMAGGIO DI CAPRA

Figs with Goats' Cheese

The best figs for this recipe are the purple ones. Do not peel them if they are very ripe, just put them in the refrigerator for about two hours before serving.

18 purple figs
210 g/7 oz semi-fresh goats' cheese
210 g/7 oz watercress, rocket (arugula) or mâche
4 tbsp extra virgin olive oil
3 tbsp pine nuts
Salt and pepper

Halve the figs vertically, then arrange on a serving platter. Crumble the goats' cheese on top of the figs. Wash and dry the salad greens, and arrange around the figs.
Combine the oil with salt and pepper to taste. Pour over the salad and figs. Sprinkle with the pine nuts. Serve immediately.
Serves 6.

ROTOLINI DI SALMONE AI CAPRINI

Smoked Salmon Rolls with Goats' Cheese

If you cannot find goats' cheese, use ricotta cheese, although it is less tasty. Sometimes I add a couple of tablespoons of black or red caviar or lumpfish roe for a more unusual dish.

210 g/7 oz fresh goats' cheese
1 tbsp grated fresh horseradish
1 tbsp lemon juice
2 tbsp extra virgin olive oil
2 tbsp double (heavy) cream
1 tbsp finely chopped onion
6 large smoked salmon slices
210 g/7 oz lettuce

Beat the goats' cheese with the horseradish, lemon juice, olive oil, cream and onion until well blended. Divide the mixture between the salmon slices, and roll up to form 6 cylinders. Cut each cylinder into 3 slices. Tear the lettuce and arrange on a serving platter. Top with the salmon rolls. Serve at room temperature.
Serves 6.

HOT FORK FOOD
PESCI, VERDURE, POLLAME

DURING THE CHILLY MONTHS OF THE YEAR IT IS OFTEN MORE SATISFYING TO BEGIN A DINNER PARTY WITH A HOT ANTIPASTO, ESPECIALLY WHEN IT IS TO BE SERVED WHILE YOUR GUESTS ARE SEATED AT TABLE. THESE RECIPES ARE FOR JUST SUCH AN OCCASION.

Warm fish dishes are relatively recent additions to the repertoire of classic antipasti recipes and have enriched the tradition immensely. I can think of at least a couple of reasons that explain their arrival on the menu. Today when many diners prefer to go light on meat, creative chefs have to come up with innovative fish dishes to stimulate the appetite. Also, thanks to the modern technology of freezing and packaging, many of the usual seafood antipasti became available at the local supermarket. When people went out to dinner, either in the home of friends or at restaurants, they looked forward to something more unusual to begin the meal. Seafood of all types, often combined with just a single complementary ingredient and served warm is a wonderful way to meet these expectations.

Fowl, *pollame*, is perhaps the meat most suited for a hot antipasto, as it is not heavy and the more gamey varieties are especially tasty. Local Italian chickens, especially in Tuscany, are full of flavour. It is well worth the extra time and money to search out and buy good free-range chickens. Chickens raised in battery farms are tasteless and require a heavy dose of seasoning to make them acceptable.

The vegetable recipes are among my personal preferences for beginning a meal. Most of them are quick and easy to prepare, yet at the same time make for a fresh, colourful and appetizing start to your meal. I am fortunate to have a large kitchen garden at Coltibuono right outside my window. The farmers' market movement in the United States, spearheaded by Alice Waters of *Chez Panisse* in Berkeley, California, and others, has made wonderful vegetables available to the city cook. Produce taken straight from the garden will enhance your efforts in the kitchen.

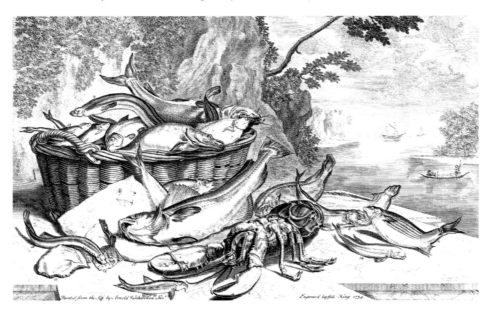

CAPESANTE ALLA VERZA

Scallops with Savoy Cabbage

This is an unusual combination that can become an elegant dish when you press the cooked cabbage into individual moulds and invert them in the centre of the dishes, then surround with the sautéed scallops with their red corals.

300 g/10 oz savoy cabbage
36 scallops, with red corals
6 tbsp extra virgin olive oil
3 garlic cloves, chopped
Grated zest and juice of 1 lemon
Salt and pepper

Finely shred the cabbage. Bring a large pan of water to the boil. Add salt and the cabbage and blanch for a couple of minutes. Drain. Open and clean the scallops and separate the red corals. Blanch the scallops for 1 minute in the cabbage water, then drain.
Heat half of the oil with the garlic in a large pan over a medium heat. Add the cabbage and sauté for a couple of minutes. Stir in the lemon zest. Cover, lower the heat and simmer for a further 20 minutes, or until tender. Remove from the heat and keep warm.
Heat the rest of the oil in a frying pan over a medium heat. Add the scallops and sauté for a couple of minutes, turning them once delicately. Add the red corals, the lemon juice and salt and pepper to taste and sauté for a further 1 minute.
Press the cabbage into 90 ml/3 fl oz ramekins, then invert on to individual dishes. Surround with the scallops and corals. Serve immediately, while still hot.
Serves 6.

OSTRICHE GRATINATE ALLA PANCETTA

Oysters au Gratin with Pancetta

If you do not want to buy oysters, a good substitute is large mussels or scallops. We used to make this when we were sailing on the empty coast of Sardinia years ago, before it was crowded with motor boats.

36 oysters
90 g/3 oz pancetta
60 g/2 oz/$^3/_4$ cup button mushrooms
2 tbsp snipped fresh chives
2 tbsp chopped fresh flat-leaf parsley
2 tbsp fine dry breadcrumbs
30 g/1 oz/2 tbsp unsalted butter, diced

Open the oysters and scoop out the inside. Pour the liquid into a pan. Add the oysters and just heat, without boiling, over a medium heat; they should not really cook, but just become a little stiff. Clean and wash the shells and arrange in an ovenproof dish. Return the oysters to their shells.
Preheat the grill to high. Cook the *pancetta* in a frying pan over a medium heat until golden and crispy. Drain and crumble; reserve the *pancetta* fat. Wipe clean the mushrooms, then chop finely. Combine the *pancetta*, the mushrooms, chives and parsley. Cover the oysters with the *pancetta* mixture. Sprinkle with the breadcrumbs, top each with a little butter and pour over the fat.
Grill (broil) the oysters for about 5 minutes, or until they fry on the top. Transfer to a serving platter. Serve immediately, while still very hot.
Serves 6.

Opposite page: Scallops with Savoy Cabbage

CECI AI GAMBERETTI E ROSMARINO

Chick-peas with Prawns (Shrimp) and Rosemary

Chick-peas take a very long time to cook and also require lengthy soaking before cooking, but I think it is worthwhile because they are very tasty, even more so than beans, and are an excellent complement to many dishes. Often I purée them with a little oil and the cooking water to make a sauce to serve with *ravioli* or a short pasta like *penne*.

300 g/10 oz/2 cups dried chick-peas
300g/10 oz uncooked small prawns (shrimp), peeled and deveined
3 garlic cloves
6 tbsp extra virgin olive oil
3 sprigs rosemary
Juice of 1 lemon
Salt and pepper

Soak the chick-peas overnight in water. Drain and place them in a pan with fresh water to cover. Bring to the boil and then cook over a very low heat for about 2 hours. Drain, sprinkle with salt and pepper to taste and keep warm on a serving platter.
Meanwhile, bring another pan of water to the boil. Add the prawns (shrimp) and cook for just 1 minute. Drain well, then add to the chick-peas and keep warm. Chop the garlic. Heat the oil in a frying pan over a medium heat. Add the garlic and rosemary and sauté for about 3 minutes, or until barely golden. Remove the pan from the heat and pour in the lemon juice. Pour over the chick-peas and serve quite warm.
Serves 6.

CODA DI ROSPO ALLO YOGURT

Monkfish with Yogurt

Monkfish is one of the most delicate fishes, but if it is impossible to get, substitute sole fillet, which should be cooked rolled.

1.5 kg/3 lb monkfish tail, skinned
3 small courgettes (zucchini)
240 ml/8 fl oz/1 cup plain yogurt
3 garlic cloves
1 handful fresh mint leaves
3 tbsp extra virgin olive oil
Pinch of hot-pepper flakes
Salt

Preheat the oven to 200°C/400°F/Gas 6. Cut out 6 23 cm/9 in square pieces of parchment paper. Divide the monkfish into 6 slices. Slice the courgettes (zucchini) paper thin lengthwise. Put the yogurt, garlic, mint leaves, olive oil, pepper flakes and salt to taste in a blender and blend until creamed. Arrange the fish in the centre of the paper squares. Cover with the courgette (zucchini) and yogurt cream. Enclose the fish in a type of parcel, twisting the edges to seal. Place the parcels on a baking sheet. Cook in the oven for about 10 minutes, or until the fish becomes opaque and white; open parcel to test. Open the paper parcels slightly and arrange on individual plates. Serve immediately.
Serves 6.

BACCALÁ AI PORRI

Salted Cod with Leeks

In Italy it is possible to buy (usually on Thursday and Friday) salted cod already soaked in water. If you are not so fortunate, all you have to do is soak it for 24 hours to reconstitute.

600 g/1¼ lb salted cod
600 g/1¼ lb leeks
6 tbsp extra virgin olive oil
2 tbsp snipped fresh chives

Wash the salted cod to remove the salt, then put in a large bowl with water to cover and leave for 24 hours, changing the water about 6 times. Drain and remove the bones. Cut into large pieces.
Place the salt cod in a pan and cover with water. Bring to the boil. Lower the heat and simmer for about 10 minutes. Drain and break into small pieces, almost crumbled. Clean and slice the leeks crosswise.
Heat 4 tbsp of the oil in a frying pan over a medium heat. Add the leeks and sauté for about 10 minutes until barely golden, stirring frequently. Add the fish and heat through for a couple of minutes. Add the rest of the oil, stir well and transfer to a warmed serving platter. Sprinkle with the chives. Serve immediately, while still quite hot.
Serves 6.

FILETTI DI SOGLIOLA ALLA RUCOLA E ZAFFERANO

Sole Fillets with Rocket (Arugula) and Saffron

Saffron, once used mainly in Arabic cooking, arrived in Europe through Spain and was rapidly accepted. In England by 1736 it was recommended for cooking in broths and with meats and vegetables because it was spicy. In Italy it was very well known by the Roman times. Apicius and Petronius Arbiter both spoke about foods that included saffron.

6 sole fillets
1 handful basil leaves
120 ml/4 fl oz/½ cup extra virgin olive oil
210 g/7 oz rocket (arugula)
Large pinch saffron threads
Salt

Preheat the oven to 220°C/425°F/Gas 7.
Steam the sole fillets or cook them in a tightly covered pan with 2 tbsp water for about 3 minutes.
Meanwhile, put the basil, oil and salt to taste in a blender and blend until creamy.
Arrange the rocket (arugula) on a heatproof serving platter. Top with the sole and pour over the oil and basil mixture. Place in the oven and heat through for a couple of minutes. Sprinkle with the saffron and serve immediately.
Serves 6.

FILETTI DI SOGLIOLA CON LE FAVE

Sole Fillets with Broad (Fava) Beans

You can buy already filleted sole or you can prepare the fillets yourself – just make a small cut in the tail of the sole and pulling firmly on the skin, the fillet will detach easily. From each sole you will get two fillets.

6 sole fillets
30 g/1 oz/2 tbsp unsalted butter, diced
120 g/4 oz lettuce, finely shredded
300 g/10 oz fresh broad (fava) beans, about 1 kg/2 lb, unshelled
4 tbsp dry white wine
Salt and pepper

Roll up the sole fillets, starting at the tail and, secure with wooden cocktail sticks (toothpicks). Place in a large frying pan over a medium heat. Top with the butter, lettuce, beans and salt and pepper to taste. Pour over the wine. Cover and cook for about 5 minutes, shaking the pan, but not mixing. Uncover and continue cooking for 2 minutes to reduce the liquid. Transfer to a platter and serve warm.
Serve 6.

SEPPIE ALLA MELAGRANA

Squid with Pomegranate

Pomegranate, a typical Mediterranean fruit, is becoming more and more popular in Italy as an ingredient for risotto and to accompany meats and fish. It grows abundantly in the south and in Sicily.

6 squid, about 150 g/5 oz each
2 pomegranates
1 large egg (U.S. extra large)
1 handful coarse country bread, soaked in milk and squeezed dry
3 tbsp extra virgin olive oil
120 ml/4 fl oz/$\frac{1}{2}$ cup dry white wine
Salt and pepper

Clean the squid by removing the ink sac and cutting off the tentacles. Chop the tentacles finely. Open the pomegranates and reserve the seeds.
Combine the squid tentacles, half the pomegranate seeds, the egg, the bread, salt and pepper to taste. Use this mixture to fill the squid sacs. Close them with wooden cocktail sticks (toothpicks) so the filling doesn't fall out during cooking.
Heat the oil in a frying pan over a medium heat. Add the squid and cook for about 10 minutes, covered. Add the wine a little at a time and cook for a further 20 minutes, turning the squid a couple of times. Remove the lid and let all the liquid evaporate. Arrange the squid on a serving platter and keep warm. Add the rest of the pomegranate seeds to the pan and cook for just a couple of minutes to heat. Sprinkle them over the squid. Serve immediately.
Serves 6.

Opposite page: Squid with Pomegranate

GAMBERI ALL' AGLIO

Prawns (Shrimp) with Garlic

This is a dish I used to love when I was travelling in Spain. I imported it to Italy and made some small changes by adding the oil and sprinkling with parsley. The prawns (shrimp) must be very quickly cooked and served very hot. I like to present this preparation on a bed of watercress when I can find it, otherwise mâche will do.

210 g/7 oz watercress or mâche
120 ml/4 fl oz/¹/₂ cup extra virgin olive oil
3 garlic cloves left whole
600 g/1¹/₄ lb uncooked prawns (shrimp)
Juice of 2 lemons
2 tbsp chopped fresh flat-leaf parsley
Salt and pepper

Wash the salad greens, dry carefully and arrange on the serving platter.
Heat the oil in a frying pan over a medium heat. Add the garlic and cook for about 3 minutes or until translucent. Add the prawns (shrimp), stir and cook on a high heat for a further couple of minutes. Sprinkle with the lemon juice and salt and pepper to taste. Let the liquid evaporate for a further minute, then arrange on top of the salad and sprinkle with the parsley. Serve immediately.
Serves 6.

FRITTURA DI COZZE

Fried Mussels

Ages ago, when the seas were full of fish, we used to pick our mussels from the rocks just before lunch and eat them raw, sprinkled with lemon juice. But sometimes, for a special treat, I like to serve them with a mayonnaise finished with a little yogurt and hot pepper flakes.

18 large mussels, scrubbed
2 large eggs (U.S. extra large) plus 1 egg and 1 extra yolk for the mayonnaise
120 g/4 oz/1 cup dry fine breadcrumbs
120 ml/4 fl oz/¹/₂ cup extra virgin olive oil
Juice of 1 lemon
Pinch hot pepper flakes
960 ml/32 fl oz/4 cups vegetable oil for deep-frying
Salt

Discard any open mussels that do not close when tapped. Put the mussels in a large pan, cover tightly and cook over a medium heat for 3 minutes, or until they open; discard any mussels that remain closed. Drain, filter the liquid and reserve 4 tbsp. Remove the mussels from their shells; reserve the shells.
Beat 2 eggs in a dish and add salt to taste. Put the breadcrumbs in another dish. Pat dry the mussels, and dip them in the eggs and then in the breadcrumbs to coat; set aside.
Make the mayonnaise by blending 1 egg and the yolk with a little salt in a blender. With the motor still running, pour in the oil a little at a time. When the mayonnaise forms, add the lemon juice and the reserved mussel cooking liquid. Blend well, then stir in the pepper flakes.
Heat the oil in a heavy-bottomed saucepan to 180°C/350°F, or until a cube of bread browns in 1 minute. Add the mussels and deep-fry for about 10 minutes until golden. Drain on paper towels. Return the mussels to their shells. Arrange on a warmed serving platter and serve immediately, very hot, with the mayonnaise in a bowl.
Serves 6.

CARCIOFI RIPIENI ALLA BIRRA

Stuffed Artichokes Cooked in Beer

Beer is a very ancient drink. In 4500 BC it was offered along with wheat and a goat to the gods in the first summer *tavoletta*. At that time it was believed to be drunk by the dead in the next world to make them feel happy. In ancient Egypt it was diluted with water and fed to newborn babies in the belief it would make them grow strong.

6 artichokes
Juice of 1 lemon
90 g/3 oz prosciutto
1 handful coarse country bread, soaked in milk
and squeezed dry
1 large egg (U.S. extra large)
2 tbsp chopped fresh flat-leaf parsley
1 garlic clove, chopped
2 tbsp extra virgin olive oil
120 ml/4 fl oz/^{1}/$_2$ cup beer
Salt and pepper

Clean the artichokes, discarding the outer tough leaves, the furry choke and the ends. Drop the cleaned artichokes immediately into a bowl filled with water and the lemon juice to prevent browning. Chop the *prosciutto* and combine it in a bowl with the bread, egg, parsley and garlic. Add salt and pepper to taste. Drain the artichokes and slightly open the leaves. Fill the centres with the stuffing. Arrange them in a flameproof casserole, standing upright close together. Pour over the oil and beer. Cover and cook over a low heat for about 30 minutes; if necessary, add more beer a little at a time to keep moist. Arrange on a platter and serve quite warm.
Serves 6.

CROCCHETTE DI PATATE ALLA CREMA DI FORMAGGIO

Potato Croquettes on Cheese Sauce

You can fry the *croquettes* and keep them hot while making the cheese cream, or let them cool and reheat when ready to serve.

1 kg/2 lb unpeeled boiling potatoes
210 g/7 oz/1^1/$_2$ cups plus 2 tbsp plain (all-purpose) flour
60 g/2 oz/4 tbsp unsalted butter, softened
1 egg yolk, plus 2 whole eggs for dipping
120 g/4 oz/1 cup fine dry breadcrumbs
960 ml/32 fl oz/4 cups vegetable oil for deep-frying
3 spring onions (scallions), finely sliced
240 ml/8 fl oz/1 cup milk
300 g/10 oz taleggio, camembert or brie cheese, rind removed
if necessary
Salt and pepper

Boil the potatoes in their skins until tender. Drain and when cool enough to handle, peel and mash while still warm. Leave to cool. Add half the flour, the butter and egg yolk and mix together with your hands. Flour the work surface with the remaining flour, and form the potato mixture into balls the size of small eggs.
Beat the 2 whole eggs in a deep dish and put the breadcrumbs in another. Dip the potato balls in the eggs to coat well and then in the breadcrumbs.
Heat the oil to 180°C/350°F, or until a cube of bread browns in 1 minute. Deep-fry the potatoes in batches for about 10 minutes until golden and crusty. Drain on paper towels and keep warm.
Cook the spring onions (scallions) with the milk over a low heat for about 10 minutes until softened. Add the cheese and stir until it melts. Pour the sauce into a warmed deep serving platter. Arrange the potato croquettes on top. Serve immediately, very hot.
Serves 6.

PUREA DI PATATE E FAVE

Potatoes and Broad (Fava) Bean Purée

I like to present this surrounded with more cooked broad (fava) beans and a very good extra virgin oil. Sometimes I also accompany the purée with toasted bread.

3 large unpeeled potatoes
1 kg/2 lb fresh, unskinned broad (fava) beans (buy double quantity if they are not very fresh, because in that case the thin, inner skin also has to be removed)
60 g/2 oz/4 tbsp unsalted butter
240 ml/8 fl oz/1 cup milk
6 tbsp extra virgin olive oil
Salt and pepper

Boil the potatoes in their skin for about 50 minutes until tender. Drain well, and when cool enough to handle, peel and purée with a ricer while still warm. Peel the broad (fava) beans and boil in water to cover for about 10 minutes until tender; it will take longer if they are older. Put them in a blender and purée. Combine with the potatoes in a saucepan. Add the butter and milk, a little at a time, stirring so that lumps do not form. Add salt and pepper to taste. Cook over a medium heat, always stirring, for about 10 minutes.
Arrange the purée in 6 mounds on a warmed serving platter. With the back of a spoon, make 6 hollows on the tops. Fill them with the oil and serve immediately.
Serves 6.

PATATE E FUNGHI ALLA GENOVESE

Baked Porcini Mushrooms and Potatoes with Oregano

Usually fresh herbs are far better and tastier than dry ones, but in the case of oregano, dried is definitely stronger. Sometimes I replace dried oregano with wild fennel for an even stronger taste, or *nepitella calamynta* for a Tuscan touch.

120 ml/4 fl oz/$^1/_2$ cup extra virgin olive oil
1 kg/2 lb potatoes
300 g/10 oz/fresh porcini mushrooms
1 garlic clove, finely chopped
1 tbsp dried oregano
Salt and pepper

Preheat the oven to 180°C/375°F/Gas 4. Generously brush an ovenproof serving dish with some of the oil. Boil the potatoes in their skins for about 20 minutes until barely done. Leave to cool, then peel and slice. Wipe the mushrooms with a cloth, but do not wash, then slice thinly vertically including the stem. Arrange overlapping potato slices, alternated with mushroom slices, in the prepared ovenproof dish. Sprinkle with the rest of the oil, the garlic, oregano and salt and pepper to taste. Cook in the oven for about 30 minutes, or until the potatoes and mushrooms are tender and barely golden. After 15 minutes of cooking, add a couple of tablespoons of water. Serve piping hot.
Serves 6.

Opposite page: Potatoes and Broad (Fava) Bean Purée

CIPOLLE ALLA PARMIGIANA

Onions with Parmesan Cream

Onions are not only popular served as a vegetable, but they also complement almost any dish or sauce. There are distinctive different qualities to red, white or Spanish (yellow) onions. The latter are the most favoured in Italy.

6 large Spanish (yellow) onions
6 tbsp freshly grated parmesan cheese
120 ml/4 fl oz/½ cup double (heavy) cream
Salt and pepper

Preheat the oven to 180°C/350°F/Gas 4.
Roast the onions in their skins in the oven for about 1 hour.
Meanwhile, in a saucepan, stir the parmesan cheese into the cream and add salt and pepper to taste. Heat through over a medium heat without letting it boil. Peel the onions and cut off the tops. Arrange them on a platter, top with the Parmesan cream and serve immediately.
Serves 6.

FIORI DI ZUCCA RIPIENI

Courgette (Zucchini) Blossoms Filled with Ricotta

Courgette (zucchini) blossoms grow abundantly on the plant before the courgette (zucchini) starts to grow. The good ones are the males, growing on a stem.

18 very fresh courgette (zucchini) blossoms
120 g/4 oz/1 cup freshly grated parmesan cheese
120 g/4 oz/1 cup ricotta cheese
1 egg yolk
Salt and pepper

Preheat the oven to 180°C/350°F/Gas 4. Line an ovenproof dish with parchment paper. Clean the courgette (zucchini) blossoms, discarding the stem and pistils. Bring a large pan of water to the boil. Add salt and the blossoms and blanch them for about 1 minute. Drain and pat dry with a cloth. Combine the parmesan with the ricotta and egg yolk, adding pepper and a little salt if desired. Gently open the blossoms and fill them with the cheese mixture. Arrange in the prepared dish. Bake in the oven for 10 minutes. Serve hot.
Serves 6.

POMODORI RIPIENI AI CAPPERI

Caper-filled Tomatoes

Fresh tomatoes should only be eaten in the summer when they are naturally ripe. They are sold now the whole year round, but out of season they have no flavour.

6 tomatoes, not too big and quite firm
6 tbsp dry fine breadcrumbs
2 garlic cloves, chopped
2 tbsp dry oregano, or chopped fresh herbs such as flat-leaf parsley, thyme or basil
2 tbsp freshly grated parmesan cheese
1 tbsp capers in vinegar, drained and chopped
3 tbsp extra virgin olive oil
Salt and pepper

Preheat the oven to 180°C/350°F/Gas 4.
Cut the tomatoes in half and squeeze them delicately to get rid of the seeds; you can also scoop the seeds out with a teaspoon.
Mix the breadcrumbs with the garlic, oregano, parmesan cheese, capers, oil and salt and pepper to taste. Fill the halved tomatoes with the mixture and arrange on a baking sheet. Bake in the oven for about 40 minutes. Transfer to a serving platter. Serve hot or at room temperature.
Serves 6.

RADICCHIO ALLA PANCETTA

Red Radicchio with Pancetta

This is a speciality that we liked in wintertime after skiing in Cortina d'Ampezzo, a beautiful resort in the middle of the Dolomites. A nice variation to the dish is to substitute bacon for the *pancetta*. The red radicchio I use is the long and narrow type called *radicchio di Treviso*, but the round red radicchio will do also.

1 tbsp extra virgin olive oil
6 bunches red radicchio
12 slices pancetta or bacon, sliced paper thin
3 tbsp balsamic vinegar

Preheat the grill (broiler). Brush the grill (broiler) pan with the oil. Rinse the radicchio well and peel the radish, do not discard. Roll 2 *pancetta* slices around each head of radicchio to cover completely. Grill (broil) for about 20 minutes until the *pancetta* is golden and crispy, turning it over a couple of times. Transfer to a warmed serving platter and sprinkle with the balsamic vinegar. Serve immediately.
Serves 6.

FINOCCHI GRATINATI ALLA FONTINA

Fennel au Gratin with Fontina Cheese

To prepare this dish, I usually use individual ovenproof porcelain dishes, and often I replace the fennel with celeriac sliced with a mandoline.

6 fennel bulbs
120 ml/4 fl oz/¹/₂ cup milk
300 g/10 oz fontina cheese
240 ml/8 fl oz/1 cup double (heavy) cream
Pinch grated nutmeg
Salt and pepper

Preheat the oven to 180°C/350°F/Gas 4.
Rinse the fennels, discarding the outer leaves and the fronds. Slice them thinly vertically. Place in a pan, cover with the milk and add salt and pepper to taste. Cover and cook over a low heat for about 10 minutes until tender. Drain and arrange in individual ovenproof dishes. Grate the fontina, cover the fennel and add the cream and nutmeg. Bake in the oven for about 40 minutes, or until the top is golden and crusty. Serve piping hot.
Serves 6.

CAVOLFIORE IN SALSA D'UOVO E LIMONE

Cauliflower in Egg-and-lemon Sauce

One of my oldest memories is of egg-and-lemon sauce served on many vegetable moulds, steamed fish or often just over boiled rice. I like to garnish this dish with sliced hard-cooked eggs and a few capers.

1 large cauliflower, about 1 kg/2 lb
30 g/1 oz/2 tbsp unsalted butter
4 tbsp plain (all-purpose) flour
500 ml/16 fl oz/2 cups milk, at room temperature
2 egg yolks
Juice of 1 lemon
Salt and pepper

Bring a large pan of water to the boil. Add salt and the cauliflower, cover and boil for about 20 minutes. Meanwhile, melt the butter in a saucepan over a medium heat. Add the flour and mix with a wooden spoon for 2 minutes. When creamy, add the milk a little at a time, always stirring. Beat the eggs in a bowl, then add the lemon juice. Take the white sauce off the heat and add the eggs and lemon juice, stirring constantly. Add salt and pepper to taste. Drain the cauliflower and place on a warmed serving platter. Cover with the sauce and serve immediately.
Serves 6.

SFORMATINI DI RISO ALL'ANANAS

Rice Moulds with Pineapple

Remembering my wonderful travels in India, I worked out this recipe which mixes India and Italy. Risotto should always be prepared with Italian rice called *arborio* or *vialone nano*, because the grains are very starchy and the risotto in the end will become quite creamy. Another quality rice, called *carnaroli*, with bigger grains, is even better, but it is difficult to buy outside of Italy.

60 g/2 oz/4 tbsp unsalted butter
1.9 litres/64 fl oz/2 quarts Chicken Stock (page 184), boiling
90 g/3 oz pancetta
1 white onion
12 handful arborio or vialone nano rice
120 ml/4 fl oz/¹/₂ cup dry white wine
6 slices fresh pineapple
Salt and pepper

Preheat the oven to 200°C/400°F/Gas 4.
Butter 6 individual moulds with a little of the butter. Keep the stock boiling over a low heat. Chop the *pancetta* and the onion. Fry them in a large saucepan over a medium heat for about 3 minutes, or until the onion becomes translucent. Add the rice and cook for a further 3 minutes until pancetta becomes golden and crispy and the rice quite hot, stirring constantly. Pour in the wine and let it evaporate. Add enough stock to cover the rice with a veil. Cook the rice for about 12 minutes from the moment the stock was added, adding more stock every minute to keep the rice always covered with a thin veil; never let it dry out. Add half the butter and salt and pepper to taste. Switch off the heat, and stir well. Pour the risotto on to a large work surface and leave to cool completely.
Fill each mould with the risotto, pressing down slightly and smoothing the surface. Cook in the oven for about 10 minutes, or until hot. Leave to rest for 1 minute, invert each mould on to an individual plate and remove the moulds; keep warm.
Cut each pineapple slice in 4 pieces. Melt the rest of the butter in a frying pan over a low heat. Warm up the pineapples just for a couple of minutes, then arrange around the rice moulds. Serve immediately.
Serves 6.

SFORMATINI DI RISO AI PINOLI

Rice Moulds with Pine Nuts

In Italy we use pine nuts in many recipes. They are produced around the town of Pisa along the sea, in two reserves; Migliarino is still privately owned by the Dukes Salviati and San Rossore was once the property of the ex-King of Italy.

240 ml/8 fl oz/1 cup vegetable oil for frying
210 g/7 oz pine nuts
1 carrot
1 onion
1 courgette (zucchini)
1 tbsp chopped fresh flat-leaf parsley
2 tbsp extra virgin olive oil
30 g/1 oz/2 tbsp unsalted butter, plus 15 g/¹/₂ oz/1 tbsp for buttering the moulds
6 handfuls arborio rice
2 large egg yolks (U.S. extra large)
Salt and pepper

Heat the vegetable oil in a frying pan to 180°C/350°F, or until a cube of bread browns in 1 minute. Add the pine nuts and fry for about 5 minutes, stirring constantly, until golden. Drain on paper towels.
Dice the carrot, onion and courgette (zucchini). Mix with the parsley.
Preheat the oven to 200°C/400°F/Gas 6. Butter 6 individual moulds. Press the pine nuts around the insides of the buttered 150 ml ramekins to coat. Set aside.
Heat the 2 tbsp oil in a non-stick frying pan over a medium heat. Add the vegetables and sauté, stirring frequently, for about 10 minutes until almost tender. Add salt and pepper to taste.
Cook the rice in boiling salted water for about 15 minutes. Drain, then mix with the remaining butter and let it cool slightly. Add the egg yolks and cooked vegetables and mix well.
Fill the moulds with the rice and cook for about 10 minutes in the oven to heat through. Invert on to individual plates. Serve immediately, quite hot.
Serves 6.

RISOTTO AL SALTO

Sautéed Risotto

A Milanese speciality, which is actually very difficult to execute properly, because the risotto should be cooked in a very thin layer and become very crusty without breaking. If you want to make this recipe with leftover rice, set aside the portion you want to use and let it cool quickly to prevent it overcooking. Incidentally, Italians usually measure rice by the handful, never by weight (2 handfuls for each person).
To make this for six people you really need 6 non-stick frying pans. They should be about 10 in/26 cm in diameter because the rice should be in a thin layer.

Chicken Stock (page 184), boiling
1 small sweet white onion
90 g/3 oz/6 tbsp unsalted butter, plus 45 g/1½ oz/3 tbsp extra for sautéeing
12 handfuls arborio rice (or vialone nano)
240 ml/8 fl oz/1 cup dry white wine
Large pinch saffron threads (about 3 g)
120 g/4 oz/1 cup freshly grated parmesan cheese
Salt and pepper

Keep the stock boiling over a low heat. Slice the onion paper thin. Melt 90 g/3 oz/6 tbsp butter in a large saucepan over a low heat. Add the onions and fry for 3 minutes, or until translucent. Stir in the rice and cook, stirring constantly, for about 3 minutes, or until very hot. Pour in the wine and let it evaporate. Add enough stock to cover the rice. Stirring occasionally, continue to add stock to keep the surface covered with a veil of liquid; never let the rice dry out. After 10 minutes (starting from the minute the rice begins to boil), dissolve the saffron in a ladle of stock and add to the rice. After 15 minutes of boiling, switch off the heat and add salt and pepper to taste. Cover the rice and let the risotto rest a couple of minutes: the rice should still have a porridge-like consistency. Pour the risotto on a large surface and let it cool completely.

When ready to serve, divide the risotto into 6 portions and press down with a plate until about 0.5 cm/¼ in thick. Melt 7.5 g/¼ oz/½ tbsp butter in a 23 cm/9 in non-stick frying pan over a low heat. Add 1 portion of the risotto, using a large spatula. Cook for about 10 minutes one side, then carefully transfer the risotto to a lid to turn over and let it slide back into the pan to cook on the second side for another 10 minutes. It should become dark golden and crusty on both sides.

Proceed the same way with the rest of the rice. Arrange on individual plates and sprinkle with the parmesan cheese. Serve immediately, while still very hot.

Serves 6.

FAGIOLI ALL' UCCELLETTO

White Beans with Sage and Tomato Sauce

This is one of the most typical Tuscan preparations. In Tuscany it is now possible to buy different kinds of dried white beans, and *cannellini* are just one variety and not the best. The very best are considered to be *zolfini*, very small and almost round. In the United States, Great Northerns are a good substitute.

300 g/10 oz/2 cups dried zolfini, cannellini or
Great Northern beans
300 g/10 oz fresh or canned plum tomatoes,
peeled but not seeded
3 garlic cloves
1 handful fresh sage leaves
6 tbsp extra virgin olive oil
Salt and pepper

Cover the beans with water and leave overnight. Drain, cover with fresh water and bring to a very slow boil and cook for about 1 1/2 hours, or until tender. Drain.
Meanwhile, use a fork to separately mash the tomatoes and garlic. Fry the garlic and sage in a saucepan with the oil over a medium heat for about 3 minutes, or until the garlic is barely golden. Add the tomatoes and continue cooking over a very low heat, covered, for about 1 hour, adding a little water if necessary; this sauce has to be quite fluid.
Stir in the beans and salt and pepper to taste, and cook for a further 10 minutes to combine the flavours. Pour on to a warmed deep platter and serve immediately.
Serves 6.

FEGATO D'OCA ALLE ALBICOCCHE

Goose Liver with Apricots and Balsamic Vinegar

The key here is to buy a very good-quality liver, whether it comes from a goose or duck is not important. I reconstitute the apricots with *vin santo*, a semi-sweet Tuscan wine, but any good dessert wine will do.

210 g/7 oz dried apricots
240 ml/8 fl oz/1 cup vin santo
240 ml/8 fl oz/1 cup water
6 slices coarse country bread
15 g/1/2 oz/1 tbsp unsalted butter
450g/1lb goose liver
2 tbsp balsamic vinegar

Put the apricots with the *vin santo* and the water in a saucepan over a low heat and simmer for about 20 minutes until tender. Drain and keep warm.
Toast the bread until barely golden, then spread with butter. Top with the apricots and keep warm.
Heat a non-stick frying pan over a high heat. Add the goose liver and cook for 1 minute on each side. Pour balsamic vinegar over the toasts then arrange on individual warmed plates. Serve immediately.
Serves 6.

MELE RIPIENE ALLA SALSICCIA

Apples Filled with Sausages

This is a typical dish from northern Italy, where sweet and sour flavours are often mixed. I like to complement this dish with a little fresh horseradish, grated and blended with a drop of double (heavy) cream.

6 large cooking apples
6 Italian sweet sausages, about 60 g/2 oz each
1 handful coarse country bread, soaked in milk and squeezed dry
1 large egg (U.S. extra large)
3 tbsp freshly grated parmesan cheese

Preheat the oven to 180°C/350°F/Gas 4.
Cut the top off the apples, and use a teaspoon to scoop out the seeds and cores. Peel the sausages and crumble them into a bowl. Add the bread, egg and parmesan cheese, stirring until well blended.
Fill the apples with the sausage mixture. Place upright in an ovenproof dish. Cook in the oven for about 40 minutes, or until tender. Arrange on a warmed serving platter and serve immediately.
Serves 6.

Opposite page: White Beans with Sage and Tomato Sauce

UOVA IN SALSA D' ARANCIA

Eggs in Orange Sauce

To make the onions more digestible, a simple trick is to soak them in cold water for about an hour after they are sliced. This is very important, especially when you want them added raw to a salad.

6 white onions
3 tbsp extra virgin olive oil
Finely shredded zest and juice of 1 orange
3 tbsp white wine vinegar
6 large eggs (U.S. extra large)
Salt and pepper

Peel and slice the onions thinly. If you like, soak them in water for about 1 hour, then drain and pat dry.
Heat the oil in a large frying pan. Add the onions and cook, stirring frequently for about 10 minutes until barely golden. Lower the heat and continue cooking, covered, for about 2 hours, adding water all the time to keep them moist. Add salt and pepper to taste.
Put the onions in a blender with the orange juice and blend until a smooth sauce forms. Blanch the zest for about 3 minutes, then drain and keep warm.
Bring a large saucepan of water to the simmer. Add the vinegar and break the eggs into it very delicately. Simmer for a couple of minutes, or until the whites set. Pour the sauce on to a warmed serving platter. Drain the eggs with a slotted spoon and arrange them on the sauce. Sprinkle with the zest and serve immediately, while still quite warm.
Serves 6.

CROSTATINE DI MELE E FORMAGGIO DI CAPRA

Apple and Goats' Cheese Tarts

In Italian homes, we rarely serve food on individual dishes, but sometimes I do when I need a special presentation. This tart, however, can also be baked in a 27.5 cm/11 in flan tin (tart pan) with a removable bottom.

8 oz/240 g/2 cups plain (all-purpose) flour
120 g/4 oz/1 stick unsalted butter, diced
1 egg yolk
2 tbsp milk
2 tbsp honey
2 Red Delicious apples
210 g/7 oz fresh goats' cheese

Use the flour, butter, egg yolk and milk to make shortcrust (pie crust) pastry following the recipe for *Pasta Frolla* (page 182).
Preheat the oven to 180°C/350°F/Gas 4. Line a baking sheet with parchment paper.
Roll out the pastry until about 0.2 cm/$\frac{1}{8}$ in thick. Cut out six 10 cm/4 in rounds with a pastry (biscuit) cutter. Arrange on the prepared baking sheet. Prick with a fork and bake for about 30 minutes, or until barely golden. If the edges curl, remove from the oven and press flat with your hand. Leave to cool on a wire rack. Spread the honey on top of the pastry rounds. Peel, quarter and slice the apples paper thin. Arrange the slices on the pastry bases. Slice the cheese and arrange on the apples.
Preheat the grill (broiler) to high. When ready to serve, pass the tarts under the grill (broiler) for a few minutes, just until the cheese starts to melt. Arrange on individual plates and serve immediately.
Serves 6.

FEGATINI DI POLLO ALL'UVA

Chicken Livers with Grapes

Fruit with meat and fish was a Renaissance speciality once forgotten, but now popular again thanks to recent research into the cuisine of these times. The chicken livers can be replaced with small pieces of chicken breasts.

500 g/1 lb chicken livers, trimmed
500 g/1 lb white grapes
30 g/1 oz/2 tbsp unsalted butter
2 tbsp extra virgin olive oil
2 tbsp plain (all-purpose) flour
4 tbsp vin santo or semi-sweet sherry
Salt and pepper

Clean the livers and cut them in bite-size pieces. Peel the grapes, halve them and discard the seeds.
Melt the butter with the oil in a frying pan over a high heat. Add the livers and sprinkle with the flour, then cook for about 3 minutes, stirring occasionally. Add the grapes, and cook for 2 minutes longer. Stir in the *vin santo* and salt and pepper to taste and let cook for a minute until the liquid evaporates. Transfer to a warmed serving platter. Serve immediately.
Serves 6.

PETTO D'ANATRA ALLE PRUGNE

Duck Breasts with Prunes

Sometimes I replace the prunes with dried apricots, and instead of soaking the prunes or apricots in the orange juice I soak them in *vin santo* or any good dessert wine for a more tasty preparation.

18 prunes
Finely shredded zest and juice of 3 oranges
30 g/1 oz/2 tbsp unsalted butter
2 tbsp extra virgin olive oil
6 halved duck breasts (3 whole breasts)
Salt and pepper

Put the prunes in a bowl, cover with the orange juice and leave to stand for a couple of hours. Drain and reserve the juice.
Bring a small saucepan of water to the boil. Add the orange zest and boil for a couple of minutes. Drain. Melt the butter with the oil in a frying pan over a high heat. Add the duck breasts and sauté for a couple of minutes on each side. Drain and reserve, keeping them warm. Pour the orange juice into the pan and reduce over a medium heat for a couple of minutes. Add the prunes to the orange juice and cook for a further few minutes until the prunes are warm and the juice slightly syrupy. Add salt and pepper to taste. Arrange the breasts on a warmed serving platter, and cover with the prunes and the juice.
Serve immediately.
Serves 6.

PART IV

PRESERVES & BASICS

Sottoli, *literally "under oil", and* sottaceti, *"under vinegar", are foods, mostly vegetables, such as artichokes, carrots, cucumbers, onions, mushrooms, peppers and of course, olives, preserved respectively in olive oil and red or white wine vinegar.*

Traditionally they are served as part of an antipasto or as a garnish for other dishes, usually cured and cold meats. These preserves are easy to prepare and useful to have on hand in your pantry. Some Italian commercial companies produce superior garnishes, along with other fine foods. Too often, however, the brands found on market shelves use low-quality oil and vinegar which ruins the taste. It is far better to make your own with high-quality ingredients.

I have also included some recipes for the basic sauces, breads and pastry doughs. You might find it useful to consult these when you are preparing antipasti. Always keep in mind that tasteless bread or an inferior mayonnaise will detract from the best prepared antipasto, whereas high-quality, fresh, flavourful ingredients will enhance every dish.

OLIVE IN SALAMOIA

Olives in Brine

This recipe was given to me by Maro Gorki, a wonderful friend who lives nearby. She is a painter like her famous father, Arshile, an excellent gardener and a cook. Olives have a very bitter taste, so before preserving they must be pricked abundantly with a needle and kept in a bowl under running water for about three days. Otherwise you have to change the water every day for 15 days. You can use green or black olives.

1 kg/2 lb olives
960 ml/32 fl oz/4 cups water
120 g/4 oz/7 tbsp salt
3 bay leaves
1 tbsp fennel seeds

Do not stone (pit) the olives. Drain from the soaking water (see introduction, above). Add the salt to the water and bring to the boil. Add the olives and cook for a couple of minutes. Drain, reserving the water.
Place the olives in a large glass jar. Add the cloves and fennel seeds, then pour over the water and close with a lid. Store in a cool, dark place. These will be ready to serve after a month and will keep for up to 1 year. To serve, rinse with a little water, put in a bowl and add a little olive oil and grated lemon or orange zest.
Makes 1 kg/2 lb.

CARCIOFINI SOTT'OLIO

Artichokes in Oil

In Italy, artichokes are in season between October and June, and there are many variations, some smaller and some bigger. When they are very small and young they do not have the furry choke and they are at their tenderest. They can also have leaves with or without thorns.

Juice of 1 lemon
1 kg/2 lb quite small artichokes
960 ml/32 fl oz/4 cups white wine vinegar
2 bay leaves
1 tsp black peppercorns
3 cloves
About 240 ml/8 fl oz/1 cup extra virgin olive oil
Salt

Fill a bowl with water and add the lemon juice. Discard any outer hard leaves and the furry chokes of the artichokes and trim the tops, then drop in the bowl. Bring the vinegar to the boil in a large saucepan. Add 1 bay leaf, half the peppercorns, the cloves and salt to taste. Drain the artichokes and add them; if they are too big, cut them in half. Let them boil for 5 minutes, then drain and keep wrapped in a cloth to prevent browning.
When they are cold and dry, arrange them in a large glass jar with the other bay leaf and the remaining peppercorns. Pour over the oil; depending on how you arrange them in the jar they will need more or less oil, but they must be completely covered. The next few days, control the oil level, adding more if necessary. Cover with the lid and put in a cool, dark place. These will keep for about 1 year.
Makes about 750 g/24 oz.

Opposite page: Artichokes in Oil

PEPERONI SOTT'OLIO

Yellow or Red (Bell) Peppers in Oil

If you do not like the taste of the anchovy leave it out, but don't leave out the capers as they are essential for the special taste of these (bell) peppers.

1 kg/2 lb red or yellow (bell) peppers
960 ml/32 fl oz/4 cups white wine vinegar
120 g/4 oz/³/₄ cup capers in salt or vinegar
120 g/4 oz anchovy fillets in oil
About 240 ml/8 fl oz/1 cup extra virgin olive oil

Halve the (bell) peppers, discard the cores and seeds and slice lengthwise. Bring the vinegar to the boil in a large saucepan. Add the peppers and cook for a couple of minutes. Drain and let them dry and cool in a cloth. Rinse and dry the capers to get rid of the salt. Drain the anchovy fillets.
Layer the (bell) peppers with the capers and anchovies in a glass jar. Press down slightly, then add enough oil to cover. Close with a lid and keep in a cool, dark place. These will be ready to serve after a month and will keep for up to 1 year. After a couple of days, check the oil level and add more if necessary to keep the peppers covered. When ready to serve, serve with a little chopped garlic and fresh basil leaves.
Makes about 750 g/1¹/₂ lb.

FUNGHI SOTT'OLIO

Porcini Mushrooms in Oil

In Italy, we use only *porcini* mushrooms, but the highly prized *porcini* grow in damp soil between June and November when the weather is warm. You can use this procedure to preserve any variety of mushroom.

1 kg/2 lb very small porcini mushrooms
960 ml/32 fl oz/4 cups white wine vinegar
1 tsp black peppercorns
2 bay leaves
1 clove
500 ml/16 fl oz/2 cups extra virgin olive oil
Salt

Wipe the mushrooms clean but do not wash them. Bring the vinegar to the boil, then add the mushrooms and let them cook for a couple of minutes. Drain, leave to cool and dry in a cloth. Place the mushrooms in a large glass jar and add the peppercorns, bay leaves and clove. Sprinkle with salt to taste and cover completely with the oil. Close with a lid and check after a couple of days that they are still covered in oil; if not add more oil. Store them in a cook, dark place. They will be ready to serve after a month and will keep for up to 1 year.
Makes about 1 kg/2 lb.

CAVOLFIORI SOTT'ACETO

Cauliflower in Vinegar

Use only the florets, removing the stems which are more suitable for flavouring a soup. For this recipe you can also use broccoli, but in that case only boil the florets for one minute.

2 kg/4 lb cauliflower
Zest and juice of 1 lemon
500 ml/16 fl oz/2 cups white wine vinegar
1 tsp black peppercorns
2 bay leaves
Salt

Cut away the florets from the cauliflower. Bring a large pan of water to the boil. Add the lemon zest and juice, salt and the florets, and boil for a couple of minutes. Drain and leave to dry wrapped in a cloth. When the florets are cool and dry, arrange them in a large glass jar. Put the vinegar in a saucepan with the peppercorns and bay leaves and boil for a couple of minutes. Pour over the florets to cover completely. Cover with a non-metallic lid and keep in a cool, dark place. They will be ready to serve after about a month and will keep for up to 1 year.
Makes about 1 kg/2 lb.

Opposite page: Yellow or Red (Bell) Peppers in Oil

CAROTE SOTT'ACETO

Carrots in Vinegar

These are delicious served with an antipasto of ham and salami, or they can be chopped very finely and used as an ingredient for sauces or mayonnaise.

1 kg/2 lb carrots
1 handful fresh mint leaves
1 tsp granulated sugar
1 tsp black peppercorns
500 ml/16 fl oz/2 cups white wine vinegar
Salt

Peel the carrots, then slice them about 1 cm/$^1/_2$ in thick. Bring a large pan of water to the boil. Add salt and the carrots and boil for about 5 minutes. Drain and leave them to cool wrapped in a towel.
When the carrots are cold and dry, arrange them in a large glass jar. Add the mint leaves, the sugar and peppercorns. Cover completely with the vinegar. Close them with a non-metallic lid and keep in a cool, dark place. They will be ready to serve after about a month and will keep for up to 1 year.
Makes about 1 kg/2 lb.

CETRIOLI SOTT'ACETO

Cucumbers in Vinegar

The best cucumbers to preserve in vinegar are the very small ones, no larger than a child's finger. But if you cannot find them because they are such a special variety, use cucumbers a little larger, but remember they must be completely covered with vinegar in the jar, so be careful about the size.

1 kg/2 lb unpeeled tiny cucumbers
960 ml/32 fl oz/4 cups white wine vinegar
3 garlic cloves
1 handful mint leaves
Salt

Scrub the cucumbers and place in a large bowl. Cover with salt and leave for about 12 hours, stirring delicately from time to time.
Rinse the cucumbers then dry them in a cloth. Put in a large glass jar. Put the vinegar in a saucepan with the garlic cloves and mint leaves and boil for a couple of minutes. Pour over the cucumbers to cover completely. Close with a non-metallic lid and keep them in a cool, dark place. They will be ready to serve after a month and will keep for up to 1 year.
Makes about 1 kg/2 lb.

CIPOLLINE IN AGRODOLCE

Baby Onions in Sweet-and-sour Sauce

These are particularly suitable as antipasti to surround tartare or meat *carpaccio*. The best-quality onions are flat on top and quite small.

1 kg/2 lb baby onions, all about the same size
15 g/$^1/_2$ oz/1 tbsp unsalted butter
2 tbsp extra virgin olive oil
3 tbsp granulated sugar
120 m/4 fl oz/$^1/_2$ cup white wine vinegar
120 ml/4 fl oz/$^1/_2$ cup dry white wine
2 cloves
2 bay leaves
Salt and pepper

Peel the onions. Melt the butter with the oil in a large frying pan over a high heat. Add the sugar and stir constantly until brown. Add the onions and sauté for a couple of minutes. Pour in the vinegar and wine and add the cloves, bay leaves and salt and pepper to taste.
Lower the heat and cook, uncovered, for about 10 minutes stirring occasionally, or until tender; the liquid should be reduced to a couple of spoonfuls, if not, drain the onions and reduce the liquid over a low heat. Place the onions in a preserving jar and pour the reserved liquid over. Close the lid tightly. Put the jar in a large saucepan and cover completely with water. Boil for about 15 minutes. Leave to cool in the water. Remove and store in a cool, dark place. They will be ready to use immediately and can be kept for up to 3 months.
Makes about 1 kg/2 lb.

MAIONESE

Mayonnaise

Mayonnaise should be fairly thick, because you can always dilute it with a little milk or lemon juice if necessary, but remember that this will also dilute the flavour. You can make it in a food processor or by hand.

Food processor method:
1 large egg and 1 large yolk (U.S. extra large)
200 ml/7 fl oz/³/₄ cup plus 2 tbsp extra virgin olive oil
Salt

Put the whole egg and the yolk in a food processor, add the salt and blend briefly. Gradually, with the motor running, add the oil in a steady stream.
Makes about 240 ml/8 fl oz/1 cup.

Hand method:
1 large egg yolk (U.S. extra large)
6 tbsp extra virgin olive oil
Salt

Put the yolk in a small bowl. Add a little salt and beat with a wooden spoon for a minute. Add the oil, a very little at a time in a steady stream, always stirring quite slowly at the beginning, then a little faster at the end, until the mayonnaise forms.
Makes about 180 ml/6 fl oz/³/₄ cup.

BESCIAMELLA

White Sauce

This is a sauce used frequently in Italian cooking: in lasagne, with baking polenta and in *timbales*. If you add the milk a little at a time the sauce is less likely to form lumps.

30 g/1 oz/2 tbsp unsalted butter
30 g/1 oz/4 tbsp plain (all-purpose) flour
300 ml/10 fl oz/1 cup plus 2 tbsp milk
Salt and pepper

Melt the butter in a saucepan over a medium heat. Add the flour and stir with a wooden spoon for a couple of minutes until well blended. Gradually stir in the milk, waiting until each addition is incorporated before adding more; the milk can be cold or at room temperature. This quantity of milk will make a not-too-stiff sauce – add more milk for a runnier sauce, or less for a thicker sauce.
Makes about 300 ml/10 fl oz/1¹/₄ cups.

SALSA DI POMODORO

Tomato Sauce

In Italy the custom is to use canned tomatoes for making sauces because tomatoes are usually very ripe and tasty when canned, and better than the ones you can buy which are ripened in refrigerators, rather than in the sun. In August and September, you will see lots of people in the fields picking the tomatoes for canning. I recommend using Italian canned tomatoes for this recipe. In summer, you could use peeled, fresh, ripe plum tomatoes, but do not seed these.

3 garlic cloves
6 tbsp extra virgin olive oil
1 kg/2 lb canned tomatoes or ripe plum tomatoes
Herbs (optional)
Salt and pepper

Mash the garlic with a fork. Heat the garlic and oil in a saucepan over a medium heat for about 3 minutes, until the garlic becomes translucent. Add the tomatoes, lower the heat and simmer, covered, until all the liquid has evaporated, about 1 hour; the sauce should become quite thick. At this point you can add some herbs, such as basil, thyme, flat-leaf parsley or oregano, fresh or dry at your choice. Sprinkle with salt and pepper to taste. You can keep the sauce for about three days in the refrigerator. It is impossible to give the exact amount of sauce because it depends how watery the tomatoes are.

RAGÚ DI CARNE

Meat Sauce

The cardinal rules at Coltibuono for making a good meat *ragú* are that the meat must first be browned in small pieces and then finely chopped before the cooking is finished. The sauce should cook for at least a couple of hours on a very low simmer.

210 g/7 oz boneless stewing veal
210 g/7 oz boneless stewing pork
90 g/3 oz Italian sweet sausages
30 g/1 oz/2 tbsp unsalted butter
2 tbsp extra virgin olive oil
60 g/2 oz pancetta
1 small onion, chopped
1 carrot, chopped
1 celery stalk, chopped
1 tbsp chopped flat-leaf parlsey
1 bay leaf
120 ml/4 fl oz/$^1/_2$ cup dry white wine
300 g/10 oz chopped canned tomatoes or fresh, peeled and chopped
Salt and pepper

Dice the veal and pork. Remove the casings from the sausages and crumble.
Melt the butter with the oil in a large saucepan over a medium heat. Add the *pancetta* and onion and fry for about 3 minutes until the onion is translucent and the *pancetta* is crisp. Add the meats, sausages, carrot, celery, parsley and bay leaf and cook for about 3 minutes, stirring occasionally, until the meat is barely golden. Pour in the wine and let it evaporate. Pour everything on to a wooden board. Chop finely with a knife or *mezzaluna*, then return to the pan. Add the tomatoes and salt and pepper to taste. Cover and bring to the boil, then lower the heat and simmer over a very low heat for at least a couple of hours, adding a little water from time to time, to keep moist. When all the excess liquid has evaporated the sauce is ready.
Serves 6.

Opposite page: Tomato Sauce

POLENTA

Basic Polenta

Polenta forms the base for many delicacies. It can be spooned on to a platter as soon as it is ready, covered simply with grated parmesan and melted butter, or with sautéed mushrooms, stewed meats or fishes. Or it can be toasted in the oven, deep-fried in oil, or layered with slices of cheese, ham, sausages, a light meat sauce, a white sauce or a tomato sauce.

240 g/8 oz/2 cups coarse polenta (yellow cornmeal)
1.9 litres/6 fl oz/2 quarts water
Salt

Bring the water to the boil in a heavy-bottomed saucepan over a high heat. Add salt to taste and sprinkle in the polenta, whisking constantly. Once you finish adding the polenta, cover the pan, lower the heat to a minimum and cook for 40 minutes. The polenta will then be ready to be eaten. You do not have to stir polenta. If any sticks to the bottom just fill the pan with cold water and the residue of polenta will detach automatically after a couple of hours.
Serves 6.

PASTA SFOGLIA

Puff Pastry

Puff pastry is not easy to prepare. The most important thing is that the dough and the butter have the same consistency and are the same temperature. This recipe makes about 600 g/1¹/₄ lb, which is about double the quantity you will need for any recipe in this book, but it is worthwhile to make double quantity and freeze what you do not need.

300 g/10 oz/2 cups plus 4 tbsp plain (all-purpose) flour
300 g/10 oz/2¹/₂ sticks unsalted butter
Salt

Set aside one-fifth of the flour. Heap the rest of the flour in a large bowl and make a well in the centre. Pour in 5 tbsp cold water and sprinkle with a pinch of salt. Work with the tips of your fingers until the mixture crumbles. Add 5 tbsp more water and knead the dough with the heel of the hands until the mixture becomes smooth and very elastic. Roll the dough in a ball, wrap in cling film (plastic wrap) and refrigerate for about 30 minutes.

Meanwhile, soften the butter and, using your fingers, work in the reserved flour, blending until it has the same consistency of the dough. Shape the butter into a square.
Using a rolling pin, roll the dough into a square about 1 cm/¹/₂ in thick. Place the square of butter in the centre, then fold the corners of the dough over the butter, enclosing it in an envelope of dough without allowing the edges to overlap. Press down gently with your fingers to seal. Wrap and refrigerate for about 20 minutes.
Unwrap the dough and place it on a floured surface. Roll out the dough into a rectangle about 0.5 cm/¹/₄ in thick. Fold the rectangle into thirds and flatten lightly with a floured rolling pin. Wrap the dough and refrigerate again for 20 minutes; this completes the first turn. Repeat this step for 5 more times, for a total of 6 turns. Always turn in the same direction. At the sixth turn, after folding the rectangle into thirds, roll out the dough to the required size for baking.
Makes about 600 g/20 oz.

Opposite page: Basic Polenta

Molino Artigiano

Sabrino Giovine

via Roma 110

12064 La Morra

0173 50118

PASTA PER PIZZA

Pizza dough

Pizza dough doesn't take too long to prepare, which is why it is better to make it than to buy it frozen. I never use a machine because I think it takes longer to clean the machine afterwards. I also think it is better to use fresh yeast than dried.

30 g/1 oz/2 tbsp fresh yeast
240 ml/8 fl oz/1 cup lukewarm water
360 g/12 oz/3 cups plain (all-purpose) flour
Salt

Combine the yeast and water and leave for about 10 minutes, or until it starts to foam.

Combine the flour and salt to taste in a large bowl. Make a well in the centre and gradually add the yeast mixture, using a fork to stir in the flour with a circular motion, until a dough is formed. Lightly flour a work surface and place the dough on it. Knead the dough with the heel of your hands until it is smooth and elastic. Put it in a floured bowl, cover with cling film (plastic wrap) and leave it to rise until double in volume. This can take from 1–2 hours, depending on the room temperature. Knock back (punch down) the dough on the work surface and stretch to the desired thickness.
Top and bake at 200°C/400°F/Gas 6.
Makes enough to serve 6.

PASTA ALL'UOVO

Home-made Pasta

Making fresh pasta is quite simple – you just need to practise a bit to find the right consistency. And, because flour reacts differently in dry and damp climates you will find that for each egg you may need a little more, or a little less, flour than the recipe specifies.

290 g/9 oz/2 cups plus 2 tbsp plain (all-purpose) flour
2 large eggs (U.S. extra large)

Heap the flour in a large bowl. Make a well in the centre and break in the eggs. Beat them lightly with the fork then, using a circular movement, gradually start blending the eggs into the flour and work until a crumbled dough is formed. Transfer the dough to a work surface and knead with the heel of your hands until a stiff but very smooth dough is formed. You can roll the pasta at this point with a machine or with a rolling pin to the desired thickness.
Makes about 300 g/10 oz.

PASTA FROLLA

Shortcrust (Pie crust) Pastry

This recipe makes enough dough to line a 23 cm/9 in flan tin (tart pan), which is about the size you will need to serve 6 people.

240 g/8 oz/2 cups plain (all-purpose) flour
120 g/4 oz/1 stick unsalted butter, in small pieces
1 medium egg yolk (U.S. large)
2 tbsp milk

Mound the flour in a bowl. Add the butter and, using the tips of your fingers, work the mixture until it has the consistency of crumbs. Add the egg yolk and the milk and knead quickly until well amalgamated and smooth. Shape the dough into a ball, wrap in cling film (plastic wrap) and refrigerate for at least 1 hour before using.
Makes about 360 g/12 oz.

Opposite page: Pizza Dough

BRODO DI POLLO

Chicken Stock

Italian chicken or meat stocks are quite light and do not overwhelm the flavours of the dish you are preparing. I usually discard the skin and the wings because they are too fatty.

3 ltr/5^1/2 pints/13^1/2 cups water
1 chicken
1 onion
1 large carrot
1 celery stalk
2 bay leaves
1 handful fresh flat-leaf parsley
Salt

Combine all the ingredients with water to cover in a large, deep saucepan or stock pot. Slowly bring to the boil, then cover and simmer for about 2 hours. Strain the stock through a fine sieve into a large bowl. Allow to cool. The chicken meat can be used for a salad. Put the bowl in the refrigerator and the fat will congeal. At that point it is easy to take it off. You can freeze the stock, but do not keep it in the refrigerator for more than 24 hours before doing so.
Make about 1^1/2 ltr.

ACETO AROMATICO

Herbed or Spiced Vinegar

By adding different herbs or spices, you can have a lovely vinegar to make your salads more attractive. It will take about a month to obtain the deliciously flavoured vinegar. Use one herb and one spice at a time; it is better not to mix too many flavours.

120 g/4 oz fresh herb of your choice or 60 g/2 oz spice of your choice, or garlic cloves
750 ml/1^1/4 pints/3 cups red or white wine vinegar

Strip the leaves from the herb and place this or a spice in a well-washed and dried wine bottle. Fill with the vinegar and seal well with a cork. Put in a sunny window and leave to stand for about 1 month. Strain through a paper filter, then pour the vinegar into a clean bottle. Cork and keep in a cool, dark place.
You can use the same recipe for oil, but because oil does not preserve food, be careful with fresh herbs and garlic, which can develop mould. Do not leave a herb in for more than 2 weeks and keep the oil in the refrigerator before straining. There isn't any problem with spices becoming mouldy.
Makes about 750 ml/3 cups/1^1/4 pints.

PANE NERO

Wholemeal (Wholewheat) Bread

If you prefer, you can use wholemeal (wholewheat) bread for *crostini*. This dough rises a little less than a white bread dough. Like *Pane Bianco* (page 185) this can also be made in a *frusta* shape.

30 g/1 oz/2 tbsp fresh yeast
240 ml/8 fl oz/1 cup lukewarm water
360 g/12 oz/3 cups wholemeal (whole-wheat) flour
Salt

Dissolve the yeast in the water for about 10 minutes, or until it becomes foamy.
Mound the flour in a large bowl and make a well in the centre. Add the salt and gradually add the yeast mixture, using a fork to stir in the flour with a circular motion until a dough forms.

Lightly sprinkle a work surface with flour. Transfer the dough on to it and knead with the heel of your hands for about 10 minutes, until the dough is smooth and elastic. Lightly flour a bowl, roll the dough into a ball and place into the bowl. Cover with greased cling film (plastic wrap) and let it rise at room temperature until double in volume, which can take 1–2 hours.
Knock back (punch down) the dough and shape it into 1 or 2 loaves, about 5 cm/2 in in diameter. Place on a lightly floured baking sheet and let it rise for 20 minutes.
Meanwhile, preheat the oven to 200°C/400°F/Gas 6. Bake in the oven for about 30 minutes until the loaves sound hollow when tapped. Cool on a wire rack before slicing.

PANE BIANCO

White Bread

Making bread at home is not difficult. The only skill is understanding how soft the dough should be: the more water in the dough, the lighter and more airy the bread will be. You can shape this bread into a loaf to make *bruschetta*. In Italy when we shape the bread into a long, narrow shape like a French *baguette* we call it a *frusta*. This is a good shape for *crostini*.

30 g/1 oz/2 tbsp fresh yeast
240 ml/8 fl oz/1 cup lukewarm water
360 g/12 oz/3 cups plain (all purpose) flour, plus a little extra for the table and the bowl
Salt

Dissolve the yeast in the water in a bowl for about 10 minutes, or until it becomes slightly foamy.
Mound the flour in a large bowl and make a well in the centre. Add the salt and gradually add the yeast mixture, using a fork to stir in the flour with a circular motion until a dough forms.
Lightly sprinkle a work surface with flour. Transfer the dough to it and knead with the heel of your hands for about 10 minutes until the dough becomes smooth and elastic. Lightly flour a bowl, roll the dough into a ball and place it into the bowl. Cover with greased cling film (plastic wrap) and let it rise at room temperature until double in volume, which can take 1–2 hours.
Knock back (punch down) the dough and shape into 1 or 2 loaves, about 5 cm/2 in diameter. Place on a lightly floured baking sheet and leave to rise for 20 minutes.
Meanwhile, preheat the oven to 200°C/400°F/Gas 4 .
Bake in the oven for about 30 minutes until the loaves sound hollow when tapped. Cool on a wire rack before slicing.

PANE A CASSETTA

Rectangular Bread Loaf

This is the typical bread you buy in supermarkets, usually already sliced. It is quite soft, therefore perfect for *tartine*. If you like it with more flavour, use wholemeal (wholewheat) flour in the same quantity, but remember the crumbs will be heavier. It is ideal for making sandwiches.

30 g/1 oz/2 tbsp fresh yeast
240 ml/8 fl oz/1 cup lukewarm milk
360 g/12 oz/3 cups plain (all-purpose) flour, plus a handful for working
1 tsp granulated sugar
60 g/2 oz/4 tbsp unsalted butter, melted
1 tbsp extra virgin olive oil for the bowl and the mould
Salt

Dissolve the yeast in the milk and leave for about 10 minutes or until it becomes foamy.
Mound the flour in a large bowl and make a well in the centre. Add the sugar and salt. Pour in the melted butter and gradually add the milk, using a fork to stir in the flour with a circular motion until a dough forms.
Lightly sprinkle a work surface with flour. Transfer the dough on to it and knead with the heel of your hands for about 10 minutes until the dough becomes smooth and elastic. Oil a bowl using half the oil, roll the dough into a ball and place in the bowl. Cover with greased cling film (plastic wrap) and leave to rise at room temperature until double in volume, which can take 1-2 hours.
Knock back (punch down) the dough. With the rest of the oil, oil a rectangular 23 cm/9 in loaf tin (pan).
Place the dough in it and let rise for 20 minutes.
Meanwhile, preheat the oven to 200°C/400°F/Gas 6.
Bake in the oven for about 30 minutes, or until well risen, slightly golden on the surface and sounds hollow when tapped on the bottom. Let cool almost completely in the mould, turn out on a wire rack and slice. It is always best to discard the crust.

Page numbers in **bold** refer to illustrations.

ACKNOWLEDGEMENTS

The publishers would like to thank the following copyright holders
for their permission to reproduce illustrations supplied:

Vintage Magazine Picture Library: *pages 6, 10, 14-17, 23 & 24, 27, 32, 35, 37, 91, 109, 130, 177*
Fotomas Index Picture Library: *pages 9, 13, 22, 47, 150*
Mary Evans Picture Library: *pages 11 & 12, 19, 26, 31, 66 & 67, 108, 131, 104 & 105*
Barnaby's Picture Library: *page 25*
Advertising Archive Limited: *page 28*
Robert Opie Collection: *page 42*
Dover Publications